THROUGH OPEN DOORS

*Unlocking
the Mystery of
Soul Winning*

TERESA HODGE

THROUGH OPEN DOORS

Unlocking the Mystery of Soul Winning

All scripture taken from the Bible (KJV)

All photos courtesy of Canva.com

Find Teresa Hodge on the web —
www.LadiesDrawingNigh.org

ACKNOWLEDGEMENTS

So many have prayed and encouraged me in the writing of this book.
And I praise God for each of you! I am especially thankful for my husband,
Todd, and our two daughters, Taylor and Mallory, who
have graciously given me the time necessary for this work and
encouraged me along the way.

I am also very thankful for Brother Paul Jhant, missionary to
America's troubled youth, and his wife, Rowena, my kindred-spirit friend, for
being the ones God used to provide my first open door to begin learning how
to share the gospel message. He is the
missionary I mention in chapter 19.

But without the Lord and His wisdom, help, faithfulness, and provision, this
book would not exist. Therefore, I dedicate this publication, as always, to our
Saviour Jesus Christ. For He alone is worthy of praise! May He be glorified!

O magnify the LORD with me,
and let us exalt his name together.
Psalms 34:3

CONTENTS

Introduction

Faith

11 | GOD WILL TEACH YOU.

15 | START SOMEWHERE!

21 | GOD IS BIGGER!

27 | GOD CAN USE WOMEN.

33 | WILL HE, OR WON'T HE?

41 | IT'S ALL GOD!

47 | HUNT FOR OPEN DOORS.

A Plan

57 | I NEED A PLAN.

61 | GETTING STARTED

67 | THE PROBLEM

75 | THE PUNISHMENT

85 | THE CURE

93 | THE CHOICE

99 | THERE'S MORE!

105 | NOW WHAT?

113 | ALTOGETHER NOW.

117 | OPEN DOORS

121 | COMMON OBJECTIONS

127 | A TURTLE, A TICKET, & TEENAGERS

131 | THIS MAKES THE DIFFERENCE!

136 | REFERENCES

INTRODUCTION

"You mean, you do that?" asked a former student I happened to meet in town one Saturday morning.

Wondering about the tracts I was passing out, he asked about what I was doing. So, I told him that my friend and I were passing out tracts right then, but that we had just come from doing door-to-door soul winning in a nearby neighborhood.

This young man is a Christian, but one who, like many of us, has had little to no training in soul winning. So, he asked me what we did at these houses. I told him how we give a tract and, after brief small talk, ask the question, "If you were to die today, are you 100% sure you would go to Heaven?" He was genuinely surprised. "You mean, you do that?" he asked.

God's command to go out and seek the lost still stands. God still wants to save souls. And His Word is still powerful to do so! Therefore, I've come to understand over the years of learning to share the gospel, that all I need in order to be an effective witness for Jesus is simply...Faith...and a Plan!

Since you are reading this, you likely already understand the "why" of soul winning. But maybe, like I had to, you are looking for a little help with the "how".

I'm praying for you, dear friend, that God will use the lessons He has taught me over the past twenty-five years to encourage and equip you for the greatest, most rewarding labor of love there is on the planet...seeking the lost to bring them to Christ!

Teresa

Note - All names of those mentioned in my soul-winning scenarios have been changed to protect privacy.

FAITH | CONFIDENT FAITH

...for with God
all things are possible.
~Mark 10:27

CHAPTER 1

GOD WILL TEACH YOU.

Soul winning had long been a mystery to me. I knew the Great Commission's command to us. (Matthew 28:18-20)

I'd heard many pastors preach about the Great Commission and about hell. So, I knew that we are supposed to tell others about Jesus. And I really wanted others to be saved from that eternal punishment and have a home in Heaven instead.

I knew a lot about the "what" and the "why" of soul winning. But the "how" was still a big mystery!

I remember sitting in a seminar at a Ladies Bible Conference in Tennessee many years ago listening to the speaker talk about sharing the gospel on her airplane ride to the conference. She also told us about leading a woman to Christ at her home that year after a dinner party she had hosted.

I was in awe! She spoke of witnessing about Jesus as if it was the most natural thing in the world.

And all I could think was, HOW?!

How did the missionaries I've read about, the pastors, and evangelists I've heard speak, and even this conference speaker all become soul winners?

And what exactly do they say when they share the gospel? How do these conversations get started in the first place? And how in this world did they even know what to say?

And Jesus came and spake unto them, saying, All power is given unto me in heaven and in earth. Go ye therefore, and teach all nations, baptizing them in the name of the Father, and of the Son, and of the Holy Ghost: Teaching them to observe all things whatsoever I have commanded you: and, lo, I am with you alway, even unto the end of the world. Amen.
~Matthew 28:18-20

CHAPTER 1 - GOD WILL TEACH YOU.

As I listened to this woman speak, I thought, "I wish I could be there with someone else when they shared the gospel, so that I could learn how, too." But at that time there wasn't anyone in my life who could do that for me.

Thankfully, however, God saw fit to help me learn in another way.

Read Job 36:22. What two truths does Job say about God in this verse? Who is the best teacher ever?

If you are reading this book, you must be like me...desiring to follow Christ's command to go and tell, but not sure how that's done. Well, let me just encourage you right here at the start by telling you—You CAN learn! Anyone can! Why? Because you have the best teacher...ever!

All you need is a compassion for souls and the desire to learn. And God will teach you!

How do I know this? Because it was God who taught me!

And if you still aren't sure if you could become a soul winner, then maybe this list of motivators I've included on the next page will convince you.

If you see yourself anywhere in that list, then rejoice! Because you are right where God wants you to be for Him to teach you how to find and walk through the open doors of soul-winning opportunities that He has for you. I pray that you find in the pages of this book not only the answer to the mysterious How-to, but also the increased faith, and therefore, courage, needed to become the soul winner God wills for you to be.

PRAYER - Spend a few minutes in prayer telling God your heart's desire to be used of Him to reach souls for Christ. Ask Him to teach you how to be the witness He wants you to be and to increase your faith in Him to use you.

CHECKLIST

GOD CAN TEACH YOU, IF...

☐ *If you have lost family, friends, or coworkers you care about.*

☐ *If you want to live in God's will.*

☐ *If you want your life to make a difference in this world and the one to come.*

☐ *If you want to be an answer to the Lord Jesus' prayer request in Matthew 9:38.*

☐ *If you have ever heard about people dying and wondered how many of those souls went to hell.*

☐ *If you want souls to be in Heaven because of you. Because you lived and let God work through your life.*

☐ *If you want to stand before the Lord one day with work that abides the fire of the Judgement and have rewards that allow you to have a "present" (our crowns) to then offer back to your Saviour in adoration and thanksgiving.*

Are you thinking of someone in particular who needs Jesus as Saviour? Write their name(s) below, and any other motivator that comes to mind, as your reminders to stay the course and put forth the necessary effort to learn how to share the soul-rescuing gospel message.

CHAPTER 2

START SOMEWHERE.

I had to go to jail for God to teach me to witness!

Yep. The Juvenile Detention facility in my county was the only opportunity, the only open door, I had to be able to learn. But I knew I had to start somewhere.

So, to jail I went.

Every one of us learn by doing, by trying. My daughters could never have learned to ride their new two-wheeled bikes by sitting on the couch listening to me tell them how it's done. At some point they'd have to drum up the nerve to actually sit on the bike seat and pedal as I held the back of their seat. The same holds true for learning how to be a soul winner.

We must start somewhere. You are starting by reading and gathering information. That's a great start! But simply reading this book will never be enough.

Read Psalms 32:8. What is God's promise to us in this verse? Where must we be in order for God to teach us?

After you've gathered the how-to information from your reading, you will need to get going...start pedaling. Knowing that God will hold the back of your seat and teach you. As you go out..."in the way!"

You might have to get creative, as I did, in finding an opportunity to go and practice what you learn from the pages of this book. But be sure that if you want to go, and you look for the opportunities, God *will* open a door for you, too.

When I started my journey of learning, several of us from our church, men and women, went to the Juvenile Detention facility each Monday night to hold a worship service for the boys.

We split into four groups to hold a service in each of the four wings of the facility. The men preached, and at the close of the service we women talked with the boys who wanted to learn about how they could be saved. I did this each week for over a year. Then God closed that door for me. (A subject for another book one day.)

Which left me needing to find another way to give the gospel to those all around me who would die and go to hell, if someone didn't reach out to them.

I began praying again for God to open a way for me to be obedient to His command to go and spread the gospel. I needed God to keep teaching me and helping me to learn. The Lord then taught me that there are many ways I could share the gospel with others.

Gospel Tracts

One way is to give a gospel tract.* And this may be where you, too, can start in growing as a soul winner. Unless you have the opportunity to go to jail like I did. 😊

Before He had closed the door to the Juvenile Facility, God had convicted me about warning my own neighbors about eternity and where they would spend it. So, I got out my baby stroller and invited a friend to go with me and my girls to leave a tract at each door in my neighborhood. We went out for an hour once a week. It took a few weeks, but once we finished, we decided we'd do the same in her neighborhood.

*Fellowship Tract League is a great source for tracts. The tracts are free, but if you can give a donation, it is much appreciated and helps the ministry pay shipping costs for containers of tracts sent overseas. Here's the link. **https://www.fellow shiptractleague.org/**

So, when the Lord closed the door to the Juvenile Facility, He led me to approach my pastor about gathering a group of ladies in our church to canvas our whole city. We got a city map, and over the next couple of years, did just that. Praise the Lord! After that, we started going to our neighboring city.

Read Acts 1:8. Where does Jesus tell us He will send us to tell others about Him?

CHAPTER 2 - START SOMEWHERE.

You or I may never be called to be foreign missionaries to the uttermost part of the earth, but we can go to our Jerusalem, our Judea and Samaria. And we can pray for and financially support those God does call to leave home and go abroad as foreign missionaries. And in so doing, we fulfill God's requirement of each of us to get the gospel around the world, as well as, in our own home towns.

Giving tracts is probably the easiest way to give the gospel. You don't have to say a word if you don't want to. In the beginning, we just left a tract at the door of those houses. You could leave one on a public bathroom counter or put one in a magazine at the doctor's office. The possibilities are endless. Get creative! But don't litter. And be sure to follow any other pertinent laws.

At first, you may want to just leave tracts in public places. But as your faith and courage build, you will want to say something as you give a tract to a person.

When I give a tract, I make it really easy for the person to take it. Anyone's natural reaction to someone holding something out toward them is to take it. So, when I give a tract, I hold out my hand toward the person, fairly close to them, so that they don't have to reach for it. They can easily just lift their hand to take it. Then as they take it, I say something like, "I'd like to give you this to read sometime today when you get a chance."

As you become braver still, you might add more to that first sentence. Maybe something like, "It tells you how you can be forgiven of your sins and be sure to go to heaven when you die."

Write out what you'd say as you hand someone a tract. Practice saying it out loud 5 times. Memorize it.

But as you do this for a while, the Spirit may prompt you...I'd say WILL prompt you...to try to do more. Only then can He grow you in your ability to be a more effective soul winner.

After I'd mastered handing a tract to someone and asking them to read it, the Lord impressed on me to start trying to introduce scripture into my witness. So, to start doing that, I began to give the tract, ask them to read it, and then say—

"I'd like to leave you with this verse from the Bible—For God so loved the world that he gave his only begotten Son that whosoever believeth in him should not perish but have everlasting life." And I'd also be sure to include the reference,

John 3:16, to prove to them that I was quoting actual scripture. Then I'd tell them that I hoped they'd have a good rest of their day, and leave.

Let me tell you, it won't be easy that first, or even second or third, time you do it, but you can and will get through it. And you will be so proud of yourself for standing up for Jesus in such a bold manner! It will be so worth the initial discomfort!!

What verse would you want to quote to someone? Write it out here, and memorize it word for word, and its reference.

Testimony

Another one of the easier ways of actually speaking to others the gospel is to share your testimony, the story of how you came to know Jesus as your Saviour.

In part two of this book you will begin learning how to go beyond and use the Bible to present the gospel message. But for now, I want you to start working on writing out your salvation testimony.

Using the worksheet provided, think about and write down the answers to a few key questions. In the next chapter you will write out your testimony. Your answers should be really brief.

PRAYER - Spend a few minutes thanking God for His grace to you in helping you to know you needed Him and for saving your soul from hell! Thank Him for giving you your testimony! And ask Him to use your testimony someday to help someone else know Jesus.

MY SALVATION TESTIMONY

How old were you when you believed on Jesus as your Saviour?

When did this take place? Give the date, or the time of year, or maybe your grade in school at the time.

Where were you when Jesus saved you?

Did you talk with anyone about your need of salvation? If so, who did God use to help you come to faith in Christ?

> ❝
>
> *Come and hear, all ye that fear God, and I will declare what he hath done for my soul.*
>
> *~Psalms 66:16*

What were the circumstances of your life at that time? In other words, what led to you coming to understand your need of the Saviour?

What did God change about you or your life after you were saved?

CHAPTER 3

GOD IS BIGGER!

I'm almost sure I can read your mind right now as you think about all you've read so far. Because I know that anytime we attempt to be used of God, the tempter will come alongside us and whisper all kinds of lies in our ears, causing us to doubt and to fear.

Read Genesis 3:1. What question does the devil ask Eve?

Satan wants us to doubt God, to doubt God's Word and commands. He'll have us asking ourselves whether God *really* meant for *every one of us* to go out and spread the gospel message. He'll have us try to convince ourselves that witnessing is really just for preachers, or evangelists, or missionaries. But certainly not for me!

Before we know it, if we let him, he'll have us offering God all kinds of excuses.

Do any of these excuses sound familiar?

- I'm too shy, Lord. An introvert, really.
- I can't talk to people well. I get tongue-tied.
- I wouldn't know what to say. (You *will* know by the time you finish this book.)
- And if I did know, I'd surely forget it all.
- It won't do any good. People don't seem to want to know about Jesus, anyway.
- I don't have time.
- I'm scared of dogs. (This one comes up when thinking of going door-to-door soul winning.)
- Is it safe? To talk to strangers?

Which ones of these excuses do you identify with?

Excuses can greatly hinder our service to God. So, it is important to realize that our excuses are really just fear talking. And God is bigger than our fears.

Fear of inadequacy, fear of embarrassment, fear of being ineffective, fear for our schedules, fear for our safety...those fears don't come from God.

Read 2 Timothy 1:7. What does it say about our fear?

Moses tried to offer God excuses, too.

Read Exodus 3:10-11, 12. Identify...
Moses' excuse—

God's promise—

Read Exodus 4:1, 2-9. Identify...
Moses' excuse—

God's response—

Read Exodus 4:10, 11-12. Identify...
Moses' excuse—

God's promise—

> **66**
>
> **God is BIGGER than our fears!**

Finally, in a last-ditch effort Moses asks God to send someone else! (Exodus 4:13) His final excuse? *"Anyone else* would do a better job than me, Lord!" This has been a favorite one of Satan's whispers to me over the years.

But what is God's reaction to this excuse?

Read Exodus 4:14. Was God pleased?

Moses was very fortunate that God, in His righteous anger, didn't just say, "O.K. I'll just send Aaron, then. You stay here." How awful it would have been for Moses to miss out on all the wonder that God was about to reveal of Who He is!

And how terrible it would be for us to offer God one too many excuses, too, and miss out on being used of Him in His work on earth! I don't want to miss one good thing God has for me. I don't want to be put on a shelf and miss fulfilling God's plans for me. Do you?

Read 1 Thessalonians 5:24. What does God promise you?

Let's trust God, then, to conquer our fears for us. And trust that He knows what He's doing when He calls us to do some work for Him. Remind ourselves that He knows our abilities and limitations. But more importantly, **He knows His own power to do through us what we cannot do by ourselves.** And has promised that He will do it! He *will* do through us whatever He sends us to do in His name!

> *Faithful is he that calleth you, who also will do it.*
> 1 Thessalonians 5:24

Remember, God will take you where you are and gradually teach and lead and grow you into the soul winner He wants you to be. So, don't panic! Don't try to argue with God. Just go!

PRAYER - Which ones of the excuses in my list in this chapter have you told God before? Take a few minutes to pray and ask God to help you conquer your fear with faith in Him and His power! And tell Him you are ready to trust Him to use You as His ambassador however He sees fit.

Testimony - On the space provided on the next page, use your notes from Chapter 2 to write out your salvation testimony. Make it brief, maybe 1 to 3 paragraphs.

MY SALVATION TESTIMONY

HOW I CAME TO KNOW CHRIST AS SAVIOUR.

CHAPTER 4

GOD CAN USE WOMEN.

"Women can't witness to men." Said one of the husbands in our church back then when our group of women began to go out to our neighborhoods to leave tracts and speak to anyone who might be outside.

When I heard about that, it was as if Satan whispered to me, "Yea, hath God said?" For he wanted me to question and think, "Surely, God doesn't mean for *women* to go. That's just for the men."

The devil tries to silence us women by saying, "God won't use you. You're just a woman." And if we aren't careful, we will buy into that excuse. Especially if our own husbands are involved in some ministry work. It would be easy to just think that what my husband does, he does for the both of us. But the command to "Go" is given to each one of us individually.

In order to settle this question for myself once and for all, I decided to study God's Word. I needed to know what my role as a woman was in fulfilling God's call to be His witness and reach souls. Could God use me? And how? Can women witness to men, or only to other women and children?

Let's look at the Word of God and see what He says.

Read 2 Corinthians 1:1. Who did Paul write this book to?

Read 2 Corinthians 5:19-20. What does God, through Paul, tell ALL the saints is their job for Him?

CHAPTER 4 - GOD CAN USE WOMEN.

All saints at the church at Corinth and in Achaia, which included women, are labeled ambassadors with the ministry of reconciling the world to Christ. Furthermore...

Ambassadors go. They are sent out. They don't stay at home, waiting for an opportunity to come find them.

Bible Women & Their Witness for Christ

And she coming in that instant gave thanks likewise unto the Lord, and spake of him to all them that looked for redemption in Jerusalem.
~Luke 2:38

Anna

Read Luke 2:38. Who did Anna, a woman, talk to about the birth of Christ?

Anna told all, all who looked for redemption. Surely there were some men looking for redemption in Jerusalem. So, we can conclude that Anna told both women and men of the birth of the Christ.

Jesus saith unto her, Touch me not; for I am not yet ascended to my Father: but go to my brethren, and say unto them, I ascend unto my Father, and your Father; and to my God, and your God.
~John 20:17

Mary

Read John 20:17. Who is speaking to Mary? What does He tell her to do?

Jesus told Mary to go tell his **brethren**, the disciples, that He was risen (the gospel). **Jesus told a *woman* to go tell *men*!**

CHAPTER 4 - GOD CAN USE WOMEN.

Samaritan Woman

Now read John 4:28-29,39.
Who did this woman tell to come to
Jesus?

And what was the result of her witness
to these men?

The woman at the well went into the city and
told **men** of Christ. **God blessed her witness
with many conversions!**

*And many of the
Samaritans of that
city believed on him
for the saying of the
woman, which
testified, He told me
all that ever I did.
~John 4:39*

Women at Pentecost

The disciples were told to wait in Jerusalem
for the power of the Holy Ghost to enable
them to be His witnesses. (Luke 24:49)
Then, as promised, on the Day of Pentecost,
the Holy Ghost was given.

Read Acts 1:12-15 and 2:1-4. The
eleven apostles weren't the only ones to
receive the Holy Ghost that day. Who
all was included in that group of
disciples?

*And on my servants
and on my
handmaidens I will
pour out in those
days of my Spirit;
and they shall
prophesy:
~Acts 2:18*

Women at Pentecost (continued)

Read Acts 2:4-6, 16-18. As soon as the Holy Ghost was given, what happened?

And there were dwelling at Jerusalem Jews, devout men, out of every nation under heaven.
~Acts 2:5

Who all heard this prophesying, or witnessing of Jesus?

The Holy Spirit was given to both men and women that day for the purpose of prophesying, of being witnesses of Jesus. And as there were men in the crowd, these handmaidens were empowered of the Holy Spirit to witness to men!

Evidently, ALL of us, male and female, are to be Christ's witnesses. To whoever will listen, whether male or female.

I asked the Lord Jesus to tell me for sure if I am to go out and seek the lost and witness, or if my place as a woman was to serve Him in my home and church and wait for opportunities to witness (and only to other women) to present themselves to me. He answered very clearly in His scriptures.

God has called me, a woman, to be His ambassador, to get out of the boat (my home) and come to Him, and go with Him, to do the "impossible" of winning lost souls to Him. (Matthew 14:29)

I can go out to witness, whether to men or to women, with confidence that I am in His will. And you can, too, whether you, my dear reader, are a woman or a man!

God will use you, if you let Him.

Over the years God has granted me the privilege of witnessing to many men, whether in my home (repairmen and delivery men), or out in town, or at their homes. He has even given me the blessing of seeing several of those men accept Christ as their Saviour! It is amazing to me, but many times it seems to be easier for a man to open up and let themselves show humility in front of us women than in front of another man.

God can and does use anyone to witness to anyone, regardless of gender, for the furtherance of His kingdom!

PRAYER - Thank God that He doesn't consider women second-class Christians, but rather gives all of us opportunity to share the greatest message ever, the message of hope and forgiveness and salvation!

Testimony - Read over your testimony, making any corrections or adjustments needed. Read it again out loud 3 times.

> **"**
>
> *ALL of us, male and female, are*
> *to be Christ's witnesses...*
> *to whoever will listen,*
> *whether male or female.*

CHAPTER 5

WILL HE, OR WON'T HE?

It was fifteen long years! Fifteen! Before the Lord allowed me to see the conversion of a soul through door-to-door soul-winning efforts.

One Saturday morning, my soul-winning partner and I decided to go to one last door for the day. There we met a 13-year-old young man we will call Daniel. The Lord gave me the opportunity to show Daniel in my Bible what the scriptures say about how to be forgiven and saved. And Daniel said he was ready to ask Jesus to save him.

I was so not expecting that response. So, instead of letting him go ahead and pray, I briefly reviewed the points of salvation, asking him if he understood each one. I just couldn't believe this was happening. But it did! Daniel believed on Jesus that day and was saved to the glory of our God!

I was overwhelmed with joy as we left Daniel's house! And still a little shocked, too. Well, honestly, a good bit shocked.

But why? When I know that God does not want anyone to perish. (2 Peter 3:9) And I know that He saved *my* soul.

I realized that I had begun to believe that God just didn't save as many souls in our day as He had in other times. It was as if I thought that since I wasn't seeing Him save souls wherever *I* was serving Him, then He must not be doing it anywhere.

Then it hit me.

Maybe the reason it was fifteen years before God decided to let me be there when He saved a soul was because...

I really hadn't believed that He would! My faith was weak at best.

Read Matthew 13:58. Write out that verse here.

What was lacking in this community?

What was the result?

Before we can hope to become effective in soul winning, seeing God open doors for us to share the gospel, and seeing many of those receive Jesus as Saviour, we must grasp these truths. Really take hold of them.

Being **fully convinced** that—

- God's command to go is still in effect.
- God still wants souls to be rescued from hell.
- God IS still saving souls today, whether we know about it or not.
- God WILL use anyone who is willing to be used.
- God honors FAITH in Him. And doesn't honor lack of faith in Him.

Before God will use you, you've got to believe...to know...that He will! I mean, why wouldn't He, when it is His command to each of us to go?

> *Before God will use you, you've got to believe...*
> *to KNOW...that He will!*

And if an excuse, or doubt, just popped into your mind, put it down with the truths of God's Word. With these soul-winning promises God has given to us to keep us encouraged and filled with confident faith in Him to use us for His kingdom work of saving souls.

SOUL-WINNING PROMISES

For the Son of man is come to seek and to save that which was lost.
~Luke 19:10

What is it God's will and purpose to do?

Then what can we be certain that He will do?

If we will just keep on going, keep on trying, what will happen?

And let us not be weary in well doing: for in due season we shall reap, if we faint not.
~Galatians 6:9

Jesus said unto him, If thou canst believe, all things are possible to him that believeth.
~Mark 9:23

What makes the difference between the impossible and the possible?

What then makes the difference between being used of Almighty God, or not being used, to reach the world for Christ?

Do you sometimes feel that it is impossible for you to witness and to be able to tell a stranger about Jesus?

Then Who must you rely on to do it with you?

And he said, The things which are impossible with men are possible with God.
~Luke 18:27

And he said, Come. And when Peter was come down out of the ship, he walked on the water, to go to Jesus.
~Matthew 14:29

With confidence in God's promises, we can go out to witness, believing in Jesus to do through us what is impossible for us alone!

If we share the gospel message from a heart broken for the desperate need of the souls of men, we are promised that *some* of that seed *will* take root, grow, and be reaped to yield a harvest. Meaning *some* souls WILL be saved!

They that sow in tears shall reap in joy. He that goeth forth and weepeth, bearing precious seed, shall doubtless come again with rejoicing, bringing his sheaves with him.
~Psalms 126:5-6

Therefore, my beloved brethren, be ye stedfast, unmoveable, always abounding in the work of the Lord, forasmuch as ye know that your labour is not in vain in the Lord.
~1 Corinthians 15:58

Fill in the blank.

Our labor is _____ in vain (futile, or without result) in the Lord.

We WILL be fruitful!

Fill in the blank.

God's Word will _____ return void (useless or without effect), but will accomplish His purpose. Whenever God sends it to lead a soul to repentance and faith, it *will!*

So shall my word be that goeth forth out of my mouth: it shall not return unto me void, but it shall accomplish that which I please, and it shall prosper...
~Isaiah 55:11a

Faithful is he that calleth you, who also will do it.
~1 Thessalonians 5:24

God has called me and you to bear much fruit. Therefore, since He is faithful to do through us what He calls us to do, we can know that HE will bear fruit through us! He has called us to witness and win the lost to Him. Therefore, He WILL do through us that work of winning souls!

Not everyone we witness to will be ready to receive Christ. But Luke 8:8 gives us what promise?

We can be confident that our efforts will not go completely unrewarded. SOME of those we witness to WILL be saved! And then share with others!

And other fell on good ground, and sprang up, and bare fruit an hundredfold.
~Luke 8:8a

Ye have not chosen me, but I have chosen you, and ordained you, that ye should go and bring forth fruit, and that your fruit should remain: that whatsoever ye shall ask of the Father in my name, he may give it you.
~John 15:16

What did Jesus choose you, as His disciple, to do?

You and I are chosen and ordained to the ministry, to the ministry of reconciliation (2 Corinthians 5:18-20). God has ordained that you/I "bring forth fruit, and that our fruit should remain..." Therefore, our life and witness will not be in vain, but will make a lasting difference for people in this life and in the life to come! Do you believe that?

I am completely confident that God has called me to labor in His harvest and bring forth much fruit! I, therefore, can go forth with God with all confidence that He will work through me and bring forth fruit from the gospel seed I sow and/or water!

How confident are you?

Pick 2 of these promises I've given and write them out in the space provided on the next page. Commit them to memory to grow your faith in God's promise to use you in His harvest field.

PRAYER - Praise the Lord for allowing you to play a part in His plan to spread the gospel! Ask God to forgive any unbelief in His ability or His desire to use you. Tell Him you commit to keep learning and going and trying to be His witness with confident faith in Him to work through you.

Testimony - Read your testimony out loud 3 times. Over the next couple of days, find a friend or family member and read it to them. (This is important. Don't skip over this step. Remember, God will give you courage and will honor your courage, born of faith in Him.)

GOD'S PROMISES

My Confident Faith...
God WILL open doors of
opportunity...and use me!

PROMISE 1

PROMISE 2

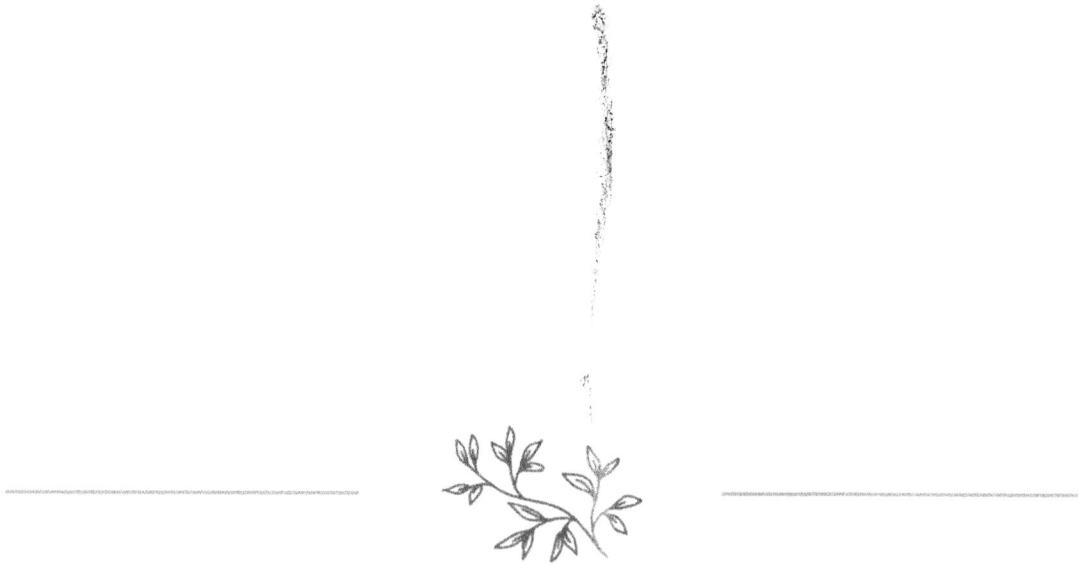

CHAPTER 6

IT'S ALL GOD!

A few years ago, I went with my late pastor and his family to a youth camp in Louisiana held each year to train teenagers to become soul winners. God had given me a love for teens, and I was looking forward to being used in His work that week. My role was to be the driver for a group of girls and take them to an apartment complex to hold Bible clubs (like VBS, only outdoors) each day for a week.

I was in awe of these young girls and their lack of fear of their surroundings. We were not in the best area of the city. But God. I felt safe the whole time. For I knew God was with us!

The Lord gave me opportunity to lead a few of the children to understand about Jesus and accept Him as their Saviour that week. Praise the Lord! But the salvation I remember the most is the teen girl in my group who got saved as we drove back to camp after club that Wednesday.

This day as I drove, one of the girls asked me to share about my salvation testimony. We always talked on the way back instead of listening to the radio. So, I shared.

This led to my sharing about how I had explained faith to the little boy who got saved at club that day. I don't remember all I told the girls, but I do remember saying that we, many times, think that we have to have "enough" faith or "the right kind of" faith for God to save us. But that isn't so. Saving faith is just taking God at His Word, believing what He said about Jesus. Giving up our efforts completely.

When we got back to the camp, one of the girls, we will call Ella, asked if she could talk to me. So, after everyone else left the car, she told me that while we were driving, she had gotten saved! I was a little dumbfounded as she was the senior leader of this group of girls. She related that she had finally understood about faith! Oh my! I had had no idea what God was doing in my car that day as I talked and drove!!

God used this experience in my life to teach me something so very important and so extremely freeing—

It's ALL God! God does the saving!

I was just driving and sharing my heart, never dreaming what was happening in my front passenger seat!

God taught me that day that it's not up to me to learn and remember just the right words. Just the right words that will convince anyone of the truth of what I'm telling them. God will take my sincere and diligent effort to share the gospel. And bring fruit from it!

This was such a freeing lesson for me. Certainly, we must learn and be careful and responsible with how we share the message of Jesus. But we aren't responsible for saving souls. That's God's work. The Holy Spirit convicts and convinces.

We do our best, and God does the rest!

I love remembering Ella's salvation because it wasn't a situation where I was trying to make sure to say the right things. I didn't later have to wonder if I said all that I should have, or if I'd maybe said too much. I know that God just did it!

Read Romans 10:14. How is faith built up in a person's heart?

Our responsibility is not to make sure WE say just the right words. It's not our words that will make the difference, anyway, but rather God's Word.

We show the scriptures and give the best explanation of each verse that we can, but it's God's Word that is the basis for anyone's faith!

And really that pressure I had put on myself was wrong of me. My faith was misplaced, and I hadn't even realized it.

Our faith must be in GOD to save souls, not in our own abilities to share the gospel in a certain way. We can trust the Holy Spirit to make the scriptures and explanations given speak to the specific heart-needs of those we witness to.

You and I are only a vessel. Only a mouth, a voice. And hands to hold out a Bible to that seeking soul to read along as we share. God does the saving!

Freeing, huh?!

This, I believe, is where Satan renders useless many of God's vessels. He gets us to take our eyes off Jesus and His power to save, and onto ourselves. Then we pressure ourselves into a total lack of faith in the gospel, which actually is "the power of God unto salvation." (Romans 1:16)

We should ask ourselves—Would I take the credit if a soul accepted Christ as Saviour after my witness to them?

And indeed, we might be tempted to...if our thinking is focused on our "right words."

But we all know that we really cannot take the credit. So then, we cannot let ourselves be pressured or discouraged with the lie, "If only I'd said something more, or something different, they would have believed on Jesus today."

We don't take the credit. We don't take the blame. We are simply presenters, messengers! We give the message, offer an invitation to receive Christ, and then leave it in God's hands. We care deeply for that person's soul, but we must remember, each person has to make their own choice.

Has the pressure to say the right things ever hindered you in your witness for Christ? Maybe even stopped you from trying?

Read 1 Corinthians 3:7. What does "the increase" refer to?

Who gives that?

We've spent these first several chapters laying a foundation of faith in God—to teach us and to do through us His work of saving souls. Why?

Because it is vitally important to our effectiveness as soul winners to fully believe that God wants to save souls, that He will save souls, and that He will use us to do our part in that work. Sure, God may use you to win some. But, with greater faith will come greater effectiveness.

Matthew 13:58 tells us, "He did not many." Which also means that He did do some.

CHAPTER 6 - IT'S ALL GOD!

But I want God to use me to do many. Use me to bring many...as many as He wants to use me for...to Christ!

All the how-to's, the best advice and tips, won't do much good without faith in God's power and willingness to save.

PRAYER - Thank God for saving souls each and every day. Thank Him for letting you be a part of His work. Thank Him that it's not any special words you might or might not say that determines whether a soul is saved, but rather the work of the Holy Spirit and the choice each person makes.

Ask Him to teach you how to share the gospel in an effective way. Tell Him you believe that He wants to use you and will use you as His witness. And that you trust Him to guide your words and to do the work only He can do. Commit to Him to keep going, and trying, and giving your best as His vessel.

Testimony - Tell someone else your testimony today. The more you say it out loud, the more comfortable you will be when given the opportunity to share it with someone who really needs to hear it!

Also I heard the voice of the Lord, saying,
Whom shall I send, and who will go for us?
Then said I,
Here am I; send me.

~ Isaiah

CHAPTER 7

THE HUNT FOR OPEN DOORS

Leigh was so willing to let me share the gospel with her and to believe on Jesus that day at the door of her mobile home that the Lord opened my eyes to yet another truth so freeing to my efforts as a soul winner. It may be obvious to you already. But for me, it was an "Aha!" moment! The revelation?

Our job is simply to go out and hunt for the open doors!

Just sow the seed of the gospel by giving out tracts or giving a word of testimony, etc. all the while looking for those who are ready and willing to listen! Just keep moving to the next person and the next and the next, until you find someone who is ready.

Read Colossians 4:3. What are we to pray for before we go out to seek souls for Jesus?

Whose job is it to open those doors?

Finally, I understood that we don't have to worry about saying just the right thing to get them to let us share the gospel with them. **We don't have to go out trying to be friendly enough, or witty enough, or experienced enough, or anything-else-enough to pry those doors open.** God has either made them ready already, or they just aren't ready, yet.

What a load off my mind and heart this was for me! I was worrying about something else that wasn't even my responsibility. And just one more way that my focus had been on myself, and not on the God who alone saves!

CHAPTER 7 - THE HUNT FOR OPEN DOORS

While it is hard when someone doesn't want to hear about Jesus, a comfort to me over the years has been to know that I've at least given them a tract to read later. I can then leave that door, or that encounter, praying for that person, praying that God will work in their hearts to make them curious enough to read it! And that God will send someone else behind me to water the seed sown that day. And rest in the truth that I've done my part for that soul that day.

So, how do we determine whether we have an open door, or not?

We ask!

I know. That sounds too easy, right? But it's the truth, praise God!

OK. So, ask what?

This question I use works wonderfully—

> "If you were to die today,
> do you know, 100% sure,
> that you would go to Heaven?"

I love this question, because even if that person isn't our open door, this question will at least cause them to consider their mortality, their eternity. It will get their minds onto spiritual matters. And God will continue to use it in that person's mind for days and weeks after!

As Mr. Frank Arthur "Bones" Jenner (November 2, 1903 – May 8, 1977) of Sydney Australia eventually discovered.[1]

I came across a short story about Mr. Jenner when cleaning out my then-pastor's office storage closet full of old magazines and papers. I started reading and couldn't put it down. I'm including this true story here, because it is inspiring, convicting, and so moving! And shows the power of using this question to find those open doors.

THE WHITE-HAIRED MAN ON GEORGE ST.

As a man from London walked down George Street in Sydney, Australia, a white-haired man stepped out of a doorway, gave him a tract and asked, "If you died tonight would you go to heaven?"

"I was astounded by those words," said the man. "Nobody ever asked me that before. All the way back to London I thought about what he said. I told a friend about it, and he led me to Christ."

This man went on to become a preacher. Years later, at a conference in Australia, he asked a woman he was counseling about her relationship with Christ. She said, "I used to live in Sydney. A few months ago, I was back there, and while shopping on George Street, a white-haired gentleman stepped out of a doorway, offered me a tract and asked, 'If you died tonight would you go to heaven?' I was so disturbed, I went into a nearby church, talked to a minister, and he led me to Christ."

The London preacher wasn't surprised, because he had experienced the same thing. After the conference he went on to preach in Perth.

After the service, he joined the senior elder for a meal. During the conversation, he asked the elder, "How were you saved?"

The elder said, "I grew up in this church

but never made a commitment to Christ. While on a business trip to Sydney three years ago, a white-haired man stepped out of a doorway on George Street, gave me a tract, and asked, 'If you died tonight would you go to heaven?' I told him I was a church elder, but that didn't impress him. When I returned to Perth, I told my pastor about this man's question, and he led me to Christ. He told me he'd long been concerned about my relationship with Christ."

The London preacher then flew back to England to speak at a Keswick convention in the Lake District. He mentioned these testimonies about the white-haired man on George Street. At the end of the meeting four elderly pastors came to him and said, "We got saved over 25 years ago through that same white-haired man on George Street."

He then flew to the Caribbean for another Keswick conference, and again told how he and others got saved through the work of this man on George Street.

After his message three missionaries came to him and said. "We also got saved over 15 years ago through that same man on George Street."

From the Caribbean he went to Atlanta, Georgia to speak at a chaplain's convention. During a meal with the

Chaplain General, the London preacher asked how he got saved. The chaplain said, "It was a miracle. I was on an American ship in the Pacific. We docked in Sydney harbor and, as usual, we sailors got drunk. We got on the wrong bus and ended up on George Street. As I stumbled off the bus a white-haired man confronted me with a tract and a question: "Sailor, If you died tonight would you go to heaven?" The fear of God shocked me sober. Back on the ship, I talked to the chaplain and he led me to Christ. I went into the ministry, and now I'm Chaplain General over 1000 chaplains all bent on soul winning.

Six months later the London preacher went to a convention of 5,000 Indian missionaries in northeast India. At the end, the Indian missionary in charge, took him to supper in his humble home. During the meal, he asked him, "How did you, a Hindu, come to Christ?"

He answered, "I traveled worldwide for the Indian Diplomatic Mission. While in Sydney, I did some last-minute shopping for gifts for my family. As I walked down George Street, a white-haired man offered me a gospel tract and asked, 'If you died tonight would you go to heaven?' I thanked him for the tract, but this question disturbed me. When I returned to India, I went to an Indian priest; he couldn't help, but said, "To satisfy your curiosity, talk to the village missionary.' I did, and he led me to Christ. I quit Hinduism, left the diplomatic service and began to study for the ministry. Now, by God's grace, I am in charge of all these missionaries, and we're winning thousands for Christ."

Eight months later this London preacher

was again preaching in Sydney. He asked the minister there if he knew an elderly, white-haired man who handed out tracts on George Street? He said, "Yes, his name is Genor (Jenner). But he doesn't do it any longer; he's too frail." The preacher wanted to meet him, so they went to his apartment. An old man welcomed them and offered them tea. The London preacher told of his own conversion, and of all the people he'd met since then who were saved after their encounter with the white-haired man on George Street.

The old man listened with tears running down his cheeks. Then he told his story: "I was a reprobate sailor on an Australian battleship. In a crisis, one of my mates – a Christian, whom I ridiculed many times – was there for me, and led me to Jesus, and my life changed from night to day. I was so grateful that I promised Jesus I'd witness for Him to at least 10 people a day. I've done this for 40 years. In my retirement years, the best place was on George Street because of the crowds. Many people took the tracts, but in 40 years of doing this work I haven't heard of anyone coming to Jesus – until today."

By my calculation, that little, white-haired man influenced at least 146,000 people to come to Jesus. I believe God was showing that London preacher just the very tip of this gospel iceberg. Only God knows how many more were won to Christ and went on to serve Him.

Mr. Jenner died just weeks after receiving this encouragement. Can you imagine the reward he received in heaven for his faithful service? His story never appeared in any Christian magazines – until now. He was only known by a few believers in Sydney.

But I assure you he's well-known in heaven. Just imagine his welcome when he heard these words: "Well done, good and faithful servant ... Enter into the joy of your Lord" (Matthew 25:23).

This article is an edited version of a taped message given by Dave Smethurst, the head of an Australian registered charity that helps Christians become more vibrant witnesses for the Lord Jesus Christ. From Grace & Truth Magazine, Danville, IL USA. Used with permission.[2]

Other Questions to Test for Open Doors

There are other questions we could ask initially. And I used to ask those. Like "Are you a Christian?" or "Are you a saved man/woman?" "Do you have a church home?" But, in the South where I live, it seems most everyone considers themselves Christian if they were raised in church, got baptized one day, own a Bible, are a good person, or know someone who is. Sounds crazy, I know. But sadly, true.

So, to get right to the heart of the matter when I go out soul winning, I now ask, "If you were to die today, do you know, 100% sure, you'd go to Heaven?" I've found that when I interrupt someone's day, they generally want me to get to the point. And that question does this nicely. (Of course, I first do a little preliminary chit-chat, so it's not quite as blunt as it sounds here. I'll give you an example a little later of just what I say when someone answers their door.)

But maybe you are talking and visiting with someone, and the Holy Spirit nudges you to turn the conversation around to spiritual matters. You might not feel right about blurting out this question in those cases. So, I've included here some other conversation starters/turners that might come in handy for you. You might also like to use one of these in special circumstances as you give a tract.

Salvation Conversation Starters

The direct approach—"If you were to die today, do you know, 100% sure, you'd go to Heaven?"

For a chronically sick person, say, "I know how you can one day be free of your pain. I know a place where there is no pain, no hurting, no sickness. I would like to tell you how you can go there, too."

For someone who has lost a loved one, say, "I know a place where there is no pain, no sorrow, no more saying goodbye. I would like to tell you about it."

For someone whose loved one has left them (divorce, abandonment), say, "I know Someone who would never leave you nor forsake you. I would like to introduce you to Him."

For a beggar, say, "I do not have any money to give, but what I do have I will gladly share with you." (Acts 3:6) Then give them a tract. Or, if you do feel led to give a little money or offer food, then do so, but don't forget the tract!

For someone who reads a tract you give him, ask, "Do you understand what you have read so far? Do you have any questions?" Then you may ask, "If you were to die today, do you know, 100% sure, that you would go to heaven?"

For someone who seems unhappy, ask, "Are you happy? I can tell you about Someone who will make you happy, if you will only receive Him."

For someone you notice was obviously under conviction during a church service, but didn't speak with anyone at the invitation time...and the Lord leads you to... ask, "What did you think about the message?"

"Do you know that your sins can be forgiven?"

Whatever the Spirit gives you to ask/say in that moment—For example, I prayed for an open door to witness to a lady who had just lost her husband. When I went to visit her she showed me a glass cross on her mantle and how she'd like to get colored light to show through it. She sat back down, and I told her that I liked that cross, too. It was very pretty. Then as the Spirit led, I told her, "But I like even more what that cross means to me." I then proceeded to tell her the significance of the cross for all of us, her included!

Practice - Choose a couple of these suggested conversation starters/turners to commit to memory. Of course, you already know #1. Out of the others, I've personally used #5, 6, 8, and 10.

PRAYER - Thank God for faithful people like Mr. Jenner. If you'd like to have a similar testimony of being used of God to reach souls for Christ, tell God so. Ask Him to help you to learn how to share the gospel responsibly using His Word. And also, to help you stay focused on Him as the Saviour of souls, and not on your own efforts.

> *Evangelism is not salesmanship.*
> *It is not urging people, pressing them, coercing them, overwhelming them, or subduing them.*
> *Evangelism is telling a message.*
> *Evangelism is reporting good news.*
>
> *~ Richard Halverson*[3]

A PLAN

SHARING THE GOSPEL

If you fail to plan,
you are planning to fail.
~Benjamin Franklin

CHAPTER 8

I NEED A PLAN.

Ok, now you know how easy it really is to find those open doors to share Jesus. But, once given an opportunity, would you know what to say?

It wasn't too many trips to the Juvenile Detention Facility before I realized that pretty soon, my group was going to want me to take a few of the boys at invitation time. I'd be called on to lead a young boy to Christ on my own! I knew I'd better get ready. I needed a plan!

So, I got a little notebook and wrote down a few scripture references and beside each one, I wrote down what I'd say about each verse.

Having a plan has stood me in good stead over the years as I've witnessed to people. I don't think I've ever repeated my plan exactly the same any two times, but having a plan memorized gave me direction when I was nervous. It also helped me not to leave out any of the really important points of the gospel explanation.

But mostly having a plan freed me to listen for and hear the Spirit's leading as I witnessed, and the person said something that didn't match my plan. I still knew what points needed to be made, so that I could, with the Spirit's help, keep the conversation on track as we went.

Having a plan also gave me confidence. I found myself becoming less and less nervous or flustered when faced with those open-door opportunities.

I want that for you, too...confidence.

Confident faith that will allow you to take the opportunities God sends your way.

Confidence that you have a plan and know what to say should someone answer your question—"If you were to die today, do you know, 100% sure, that you would go to Heaven?"—with a "No, I'm not sure."

Confidence that will keep you from having to ask someone else to take from you your opportunity to lead a soul to Christ. Faith and confidence, so that you don't miss out on that most wonderful blessing!

So, now let's talk about this plan. The plan will include an introduction and...

The 4 Critical Points of the Gospel
- The Problem - sin
- The Punishment - death
- The Cure - Christ
- The Choice - repent and believe

We will spend the next few chapters learning about how to explain each point and helping you to develop your own plan for sharing the gospel.

But for now, take a few minutes to memorize the 4 points.

PRAYER - Thank God for making the way of your salvation. Ask Him to help you in making a plan for sharing the gospel with others. Ask Him to help you in learning that plan, so that you become very comfortable in sharing it.

> *Therefore, my beloved brethren, be ye stedfast, unmoveable, always abounding in the work of the Lord, forasmuch as ye know that your labour is not in vain in the Lord.*
> *~1 Corinthians 15:58*

I'm all for lifestyle evangelism,
but I'm also in favor of intentionality,
where we seek out opportunities for
spiritual conversations and are equipped to
explain the gospel and why we believe it.

~ Lee Strobel[4]

CHAPTER 9

hello

GETTING STARTED - THE INTRODUCTION

Often the hardest part about any presentation is the beginning and the ending. It's difficult to know how to get started, and difficult to know how to wrap it up at the end. So, first, to help you get started, I want to share with you how I begin a conversation with someone whenever I go out soul winning. Of course, you may want to adjust what I say to match what is more natural for you.

But before I share that, let me say that while I'm knocking and waiting, I'm also praying! The most important part of the gospel presentation! I'm praying for God to work in the person's heart who will answer the door. I'm praying that God will open their heart and make them ready to hear and be saved that day.

At the same time, I'm also praying for the Lord to give me courage, wisdom, discernment, and the words to say. I need Him to quiet that inner voice that's screaming, "I hope they're not at home!" ☺ Yep! I still, after all these years, have that battle sometimes. But I will say that every time, as I've begun to speak, He has taken over and calmed me. So, I've learned to just "Fake it, 'til I make it." Or, rather..."Fake it, 'til He takes over!"

> **PRAYER -**
> the most important part of the gospel presentation!

Now, as I said before, I prefer a more direct approach. I've found that people don't want to stand there wondering when we're going to get to the point. So, this is what I say whenever someone answers my knock on their door. (For the sake of illustration, I've named my soul-winning partner Janet.)

"Hi! My name is Teresa, and this is Janet. We're from Grandview Pines Baptist Church. And we're out in your neighborhood today giving out these tracts (as I hold it out to them to take) and inviting people to come visit us at church tomorrow (You may need to say 'Sunday' here.), if you don't have a church home. Do you have a church?"

I acknowledge whatever answer they give, and then go on to ask my question. And say, "Well, more important than asking you to visit our church, I want to ask you this question...If you were to die today, do you know, 100% sure, that you'd go to Heaven?" (Remember to ask it slowly, pausing at each comma to let each phrase sink in.)

Most people respond with one of these—
- I hope so.
- I'm trying.
- Maybe.
- I'm not sure.

If their answer is anything other than a resounding, "Yes!" then I proceed to quote 1 John 5:13. (I'll tell you below what I say on those occasions when I'm told "Yes.")

"The Bible tells us that we can KNOW that we are going to Heaven. God says in 1 John 5:13 'These things have I written unto you that believe on the name of the Son of God; that ye may know that ye have eternal life, and that ye may believe on the name of the Son of God.' God wants us to know for sure, because we aren't promised the next minute. Life is so uncertain. **If I could show you in God's Word how you can know for sure, would you like to know?"**

That last question is how we determine if we have an open door. If they are ready to listen, then they will tell us some form of, "Yes, I'd like to know."

I then will open my Bible and show them 1 John 5:13 to prove to them what I quoted is God's Word. I tell them, "This verse tells us why God wrote the Bible! So that we could believe on His Son Jesus and know that we have eternal life in Heaven!"

"There are just 4 things you need to understand in order to be sure you are going to Heaven."

"First, you need to understand that you have a problem, and that problem is called sin."

We will cover Point #1—The Problem—in the next chapter.

So, what if the person says "Yes"?

I respond by saying, "Oh, that's great! So, there's been a time in your life when you understood that you are a sinner, and you believed that Jesus Christ, God's Son, died on the cross to pay for your sins for you, and you asked Jesus to forgive you of your sins and save you from hell?"

Or, I've said, "Oh, that's great! Do you mind sharing with us how you came to know that?" And many times, I've rejoiced to hear a clear salvation testimony.

CHAPTER 9 - THE INTRODUCTION

But just as many times I've realized that the person wasn't basing their salvation on Jesus alone. In those times, I've either tried to share my testimony, too, as a way to share the gospel with them, or I've asked the question from the paragraph above, "So, there's been a time in your life..." Just trying to leave them with some gospel message along with the tract.

I leave those opportunities praying God will open their eyes to see that they have a false security!

OUTLINE FOR THE INTRODUCTION

- Introduce yourself and those with you.
- Tell what church you are from and why you're there as you...
- Give a tract.
- Get their name.
- Ask "the question."
- Ask if they'd like to know for sure.

PRAYER - Thank the Lord for helping you to hear about Jesus. Thank Him that you know that you belong to Him!

On the next page write out your opening statement, what you would actually say to start a conversation with the intent to share the gospel message. Read it several times out loud until it sounds natural.

Being an extrovert
isn't essential to evangelism—
obedience and love are.

~ Rebecca Pippert [5]

GETTING
STARTED

THE INTRODUCTION

CHAPTER 10

THE PROBLEM - SIN

The day I met Jack out soul winning was a first for me. A real shocker. Out of all the people I've talked to over the years, Jack is the only one who claimed to have no sin!

After introducing myself, asking him "the question," and determining that he was an open door ready to listen, I showed him Romans 5:12. After explaining what sin is and where sin started, I began to ask him several questions to help him acknowledge that he, too, is a sinner.

"This verse says that 'all have sinned.' 'All' includes me, and it includes you, too. All of us have sinned. For instance, Jack, have you ever taken something without permission? Even a pen that wasn't yours?" Jack immediately responded, "No."

"Well, have you ever said something that wasn't nice or kind?" "No."

"Ok. Well, have you ever told a lie?" "No."

"So, you've never done anything wrong?" "No. I haven't," said Jack.

"Are you sure?" I asked. "Yeah."

"So, you always obeyed your mom growing up?" "Yes."

"Never were unkind to your brothers or sisters?" "No."

I was dumbfounded and half laughed out my response—"Wow! I have never met anyone as good as you are!"

Then the Spirit helped me think to ask him one last question. "Well, let me ask you this." Then looking up and pointing to the sky, "Can you honestly point your finger at God on His throne in Heaven and say, 'I am as good and holy as You are, God.'?"

"Oh. No. I couldn't."

"Well, that's the point. None of us can. Because we are ALL sinners before God.

And to go into Heaven, we must be as righteous as God is. We must be washed completely clean of our sin."

Jack didn't get saved that day, but I pray that the seed sown took root, and that one day he will understand his desperate need of forgiveness, and call on Jesus for salvation.

Read Mark 16:15. What does Jesus command of us here?

Acknowledging ourselves to be sinners against the Holy God is the first step toward repentance and faith.

Read Luke 13:3. What must take place in order that we sinners not perish?

Biblical repentance is defined as a change of mind concerning one's sin. It also involves a change of mind about who Jesus is and what He has done. Without repentance that acknowledges our sinfulness, there is no salvation. We each must acknowledge that we need saving before we can be saved.

If a person falls overboard into the lake, but believes he's in no danger, then he will never grab hold of the salvation offered to him in the form of a life ring. He must first come to terms with the fact that he needs saving, that he'd not be able to swim to shore, before he will accept help. He has to first change his mind about his need.

Repentance is the work of the Holy Spirit in a person's heart through the Word of God as we present the gospel message.

Our job as soul winners is to simply show the person the scriptures that the Holy Spirit can then use to help them see themselves as sinners before the Holy Almighty God.

There are many scriptures we could use. First, I'll give you the verse(s) I use in my plan along with the explanation I give. Then I'll give a few others along with an example of how you could use each verse. You can decide which one(s) you would want to use as you develop your own gospel plan. The other verses here could be kept in the back of your mind to use as the Spirit leads in special circumstances. That is, when the conversation doesn't go according to your plan...like what happened to me with Jack. ☺

As you share the gospel, open your Bible to each verse, so that the person can read along with you as you point to the verse and read it out loud.

When you finish reading, ask a question(s) that will allow them to answer using the information in the verse. Basically, so that they can tell you what you just read to them. Asking questions throughout the presentation will help you gauge what they understand or what needs more explanation.

Let's pretend that our person's name is Suzy. And that my soul-winning partner's name, again, is Janet.

In my plan (on the next page), I use Romans 5:12 for Point #1, so that I can talk a little about where sin came from, along with what sin is. I also like this verse, because I can stay there as I transition into Point #2 of the gospel...The Punishment.

Wherefore, as by one man (talking about Adam) sin entered into the world, and death by sin; and so death passed upon all men, for that all have sinned:
~Romans 5:12

Reading the verse aloud, I insert the explanation, "talking about Adam," after "one man" and ask, "Have you ever heard the story of Adam and Eve?" I finish the verse and then say, "God created the world and Adam and Eve and gave them only 1 command...not to eat of the tree of the knowledge of good and evil." Then I ask, "But what did they do?" I haven't had anyone not know the answer, yet. They've all said, "They ate it." I respond, "Yes, they did. They only had 1 command to obey, and they couldn't even do that! And because of their sin, everyone born into the world since then has been born a sinner. It says, 'all have sinned'."

"Sin is anything that we think, say, or do that disobeys God's commands given to us in the Bible, God's Word. For example, God commands us to obey our parents, be kind to others, and be truthful."*

"So, Suzy, let me ask you, have you ever...even once...
- disobeyed your parents (pause for her to answer), or
- been unkind (pause for her to answer), or
- told a lie (pause for her to answer)?
If we are honest with ourselves, we must all answer 'Yes' to each of those questions. Right? That's sin. And there are many other sins we commit every day, too."

"This verse says that 'all have sinned.' That means I have sinned. That means that Janet has sinned. That means that you have sinned against God, too, right?" She should answer, 'Yes.' Then say, "Someone who sins is called a sinner."

WRAP-UP QUESTION -
"So, Suzy, according to this verse, and your own admission, what are you?" She should answer, "A sinner."

*Colossians 3:20, Ephesians 4:32, Colossians 3:9

OTHER VERSES YOU COULD USE

- **Romans 3:23 - For all have sinned, and come short of the glory of God;**

"Suzy, this verse says that all have sinned. Sin is anything that we say or do that disobeys God's commands given to us in the Bible, God's Word. For example, God commands us to obey our parents, be kind to others, and be truthful. So, let me ask you, Suzy, have you ever...even once...disobeyed your parents (pause for her to answer), or been unkind (pause for her to answer), or told a lie (pause for her to answer)? If we are honest with ourselves, we must all answer "Yes" to each of those questions. Right? That's sin. And there are many other sins we commit every day, too."

"This verse says that 'all have sinned.' That means I have sinned. That means that Janet here has sinned. That means that you have sinned against God, too, right?" She should answer, "Yes." Then say, "Someone who sins is called a sinner. So, Suzy, according to this verse, and your own admission, what are you?" She should answer, "A sinner."

For those who say they haven't sinned, or that they haven't sinned that much, you might want to use one of these verses. Or, ask them what I asked Jack above.

- **Matthew 22:37-38 - Jesus said unto him, Thou shalt love the Lord thy God with all thy heart, and with all thy soul, and with all thy mind. This is the first and great commandment.**

You could ask, "Suzy, what would be your definition of a great sinner?" She will doubtless say, one who has done a lot of sin, or maybe "bad sins", like murder, etc. You could then show her Matthew 22:37-38. And ask her, "Well, Suzy, have you always loved God the way this verse says we are to love God— with all our heart, mind, soul, and strength?" Tell her "To love God in this way, you must have always loved Him above all others and put the doing of God's will before all else." If she says the truth, she will admit that she has not loved God like that.

Ask her, "Then, according to this verse, what commandment have you broken?" She will say, "The greatest commandment." Ask, "If a person breaks the greatest commandment, is she not a great sinner?" Ask, "Then according to this verse and your own admission, what are you?" She should respond, "A great sinner."

- **James 2:10 - For whosoever shall keep the whole law, and yet offend in one point, he is guilty of all.**

Say, "Suzy, you just said that you have done a few things that were wrong, even though you haven't done terrible sins." "So, you've committed at least 1 sin, right?" Show her James 2:10 and say, "Well, here God says that to 'offend in one point,' meaning to break just 1 of God's laws, makes us guilty before God."

To further illustrate, you might ask, "How many banks does a person have to rob to be a bank robber?" Suzy should answer, "Only one." Say, "That's right. And it only takes us breaking just 1 of God's laws to make us a guilty sinner. And if we're honest, we've broken many of God's laws multiple times! So, Suzy, because you have sinned, what does that make you?" She should say, "a sinner."

NOTE: As I explain point #1, I make sure to ask the person if they have ever told a lie, because that sin is listed specifically in the verse that I use to explain point #2 about the punishment for sin. Also, be sure to wrap up each point with a question to ensure that the person understands that point.

OUTLINE FOR POINT #1
- Explain what sin is and where it came from.
- Get specific by giving examples (always include lying) and asking them if they have ever done that.
- Ask the wrap-up question.

PRAYER - Thank the Lord for loving you, a sinner. And sending someone to tell you about Jesus. Praise God for that person(s) and ask God to bless them today wherever they are. Ask God to help you be that person for others.

Decide which verse(s) you'd use, and write out on the next page what you would say to share Point #1 with the person who wants to listen. Read it out loud several times until it sounds natural.

THE PROBLEM-SIN

CHAPTER 11

THE PUNISHMENT - DEATH

Read Galatians 3:10. What happens to anyone who does not perfectly follow all of God's laws?

It is very tempting to rush over this point of the gospel message in our zeal to go ahead and talk about Jesus. But it is imperative that each person understand the seriousness of the curse that they are under before they can grasp how wonderful it is that God has provided the Cure. They must realize just how great their need truly is. That they are headed for an eternity in a lake of fire!

Read 1 Corinthians 2:9. What does this verse say about Heaven?

The Bible tells us that we cannot even imagine what Heaven will be like in all its glory. Or even more, what it will be like to be in the very presence of our God! In the same way, there is no way that we can even come close to imagining the horror of hell for those who will be there for eternity. Jesus gives us a glimpse as He tells us about the exchange between the rich man and Abraham.

Read Luke 16:20-28. What does this passage reveal about hell? For example, what are some of the things that the rich man can feel and suffer and remember?

The day I came across the article about Mr. Jenner, the White-Haired Man on George Street, I also found an article about hell. The author, Joseph Nimeskern, takes many of the scriptures about hell and puts them together to try to give us a picture of the terrible reality of hell for those experiencing it today...and forever. I've obtained permission to share it with you here in order to motivate us to urgency as we explain this second point of the gospel message. Let it move you to greater faithfulness to warn the lost.

HELL'S FIRST MOMENT.... THROUGHOUT ETERNITY

by Joseph Nimeskern

Exodus 3:2 The angel of the Lord appeared unto him in a flame of fire out of the midst of a bush: and he looked and behold, the bush burned with fire and the bush was NOT CONSUMED.

Isaiah 13:8 They shall be afraid: pangs and sorrows shall take hold of them; they shall be in pain as a woman that travaileth; they shall be amazed one at another; their faces shall be as flames.

Psalms 116:3 The sorrows of death compassed me, and pains of hell gat hold upon me, I found trouble and sorrow.

What mortal mind can even begin to perceive, this side of hell, what the burning will be like. Let's see if this will give you another look at lost love ones, friends, etc., and their fate if they are not saved...maybe even your fate.

THE BURNING FALL

Revelation 20:15 And whosoever was not found written in the book of life was cast into the lake of fire.

Try to imagine for every second, throughout eternity, your body with the most excruciating sunburn. Add to that the awful pain of your whole frame scalded with boiling water. To this, add the agony of bodily movement. The skin stretches. Untold daggers of pain flash through your body. You want to hold still, but the burning from the flames will not allow it. The bubbling brimstone makes you scream. Your hair is on fire. Your feet and hands blister, while you gnaw your tongue, trying to relieve the torment. Your throat is raw from screaming and wailing.

Spasms of anguish drop you into the molten lava. You go under the surface gnashing your teeth. The burning brimstone flows into your mouth; runs down your throat and into your stomach. You are on fire inside and outside. Lava, red hot and smoking, flows in your ears. As your eyes try to focus in the endless, everlasting, permanent dwelling place of total torment...a feeling of melting of your eyes overwhelms you. You look and focus on worms that have totally engulfed your body. They are crawling on and in you. You can feel them. A scream comes from your burning, flaming, fiery lips. A cry for "Water" is felt throughout your whole being.

You are falling in the darkness. You feel something solid. Oh, if you only could stop falling! Your body tries to cling to the solid surface. Suddenly...you are slipping. Again, you fall into the bubbling lake. You swallow another mouthful of burning slime. The horrid smell of blazing sulphur combine with the sickening odor of burning hair and scorched flesh. Nausea overwhelms you.

Something suddenly reaches out of the darkness and grasps you in terror. They begin to gnash on you with their teeth. All the time you are both screaming at the top of your lungs. You shake the gnashing person off in the darkness. Breathing heavily from the concentrated exertion, you fill your lungs with smoke. While you cough and gasp, the word "WATER!!!" escapes your inflamed lips again. Your throat is on fire. Your tongue feels like a white-hot iron against the parched roof of your mouth. Your gums pulsate with agony, while every nerve in your teeth stabs you with flashes of indescribable permanent pain.

The roar of the flames and the piercing screams of the doomed and the damned seem to tear at your eardrums. Oh, for just a moment of silence! But it never comes.

You can't run away this time. Thoughts of law-abiding so-called Christians didn't tell you of this place. Additionally, your thoughts go to and fro from the time you were in a Bible-believing, preaching church. Thoughts you can so clearly remember. You remember the time when the preacher was talking to you about this hopeless place of darkness and pain. He talked about Jesus and His saving Blood...

"He told me that I was a sinner! Now I accept Jesus as my Saviour. I accept what He did for me on the cross. Can't you hear me? I want to be saved! You know, born again! What the preacher said! Won't you listen? Can't you hear?" Another scream escapes your burning lips.

For eternity you scream those words again and again, over and over, repeating these words, but alas, they go nowhere. Words, meaningless words that can't be heard by God Almighty, but by the doomed. "I want to be born again! Can't you hear me! Why didn't someone tell me! Why didn't they continue to tell me when I had ignored them! Didn't they care!" The doomed tell you it won't work. "Your words are not heard. The living and their prayers can't help. Their money won't help you here. You are condemned here for eternity just as we are." Another scream escapes your burning lips, "NO!"[6]

> *Wherefore, as by one man (talking about Adam) sin entered into the world, and death by sin; and so death passed upon all men, for that all have sinned:*
> *~Romans 5:12*

"Suzy, the next thing to understand in order to go to Heaven is that our sin, your sin, has a dire consequence. Sin brings the punishment of death and separates us from God.

Adam and Eve were the first man and woman God created. They had a perfect world in which to live. Until they disobeyed the one command God gave them. The result of their sin, and ours? Death. All people will die physically.

But there is another death, a spiritual death, known as the second death. The Bible tells us what happens to people who die this second death." (Show her the verse in your Bible, as you read it out loud.)

This is how I explain the second point of the gospel message...

But the fearful, and unbelieving, and the abominable, and murderers, and whoremongers, and sorcerers, and idolaters, and all liars, shall have their part in the lake which burneth with fire and brimstone: which is the second death. ~Revelation 21:8

"The person who dies this second death is cast into a lake a fire. Imagine being cast into a lake of molten lava. But the torment and agony of the pain experienced there isn't even the worst part about this place called hell. The souls in hell are also separated from God...and all that He is. God is love. There is no love in hell. God is light. There is no light in hell. God is good. There is no goodness, mercy, or help in hell."

WRAP-UP QUESTION -
"You've admitted that you have lied and sinned. Then according to this verse, where are you headed? If you died right now, where would you go?"

Then I continue with...

"But, Suzy, there's one more thing that you need to know about hell."

And these shall go away into everlasting punishment: but the righteous into life eternal. ~Matthew 25:46

"The punishment of hell is forever. There is no hope of escape, no second chance.

That, I believe, is the worst part about hell...*no* hope."

OTHER VERSES YOU COULD USE

- **Romans 6:23 For the wages of sin is death; but the gift of God is eternal life through Jesus Christ our Lord.**

You might say, "When we work a job, we earn wages, a paycheck. We deserve it. What we earn or deserve because of sin against God is death. We all die physically, but there is also a second death, a spiritual death. And that is what this verse is talking about. Eternal life and eternal death. Let's see what the Bible tells us about those who die this second death." Then turn to Revelation 21:8, and use the explanation above.

- **Ezekiel 18:4b …the soul that sinneth, it shall die.**

You might say, "God says that the punishment for sin is death. We all die physically, right? Cemeteries remind us of this fact. But there is another death, too, a spiritual death. Let's see what the Bible tells us about those who die this second death." Then turn to Revelation 21:8, and use the explanation above.

I don't like to think about hell. And I'm sure you don't either.

To think of loved ones that I am reasonably sure are even now, and forever, experiencing the unimaginable pain, torment, and hopelessness of hell is just too unbearable.

But, if we would force ourselves to spend just a moment each day contemplating the reality of hell, we'd be driven to go and warn the lost who still have a chance!

We'd warn those we meet throughout our day by giving tracts. We'd even go out seeking opportunities to tell others about Jesus and His so-great salvation!

And we'd be able to say with Paul…

"For though I preach the gospel, I have nothing to glory of: for necessity is laid upon me; yea, **woe is unto me, if I preach not the gospel!**" 1 Corinthians 9:16

OUTLINE FOR POINT #2
- Explain the consequence for sin—death, both physical and spiritual.
- Explain the second death in hell.
- Show that hell is everlasting.
- Ask the wrap-up question.

PRAYER - Spend time thanking and praising God with all your heart for delivering you from such a fate as hell! Ask Him to help you when you explain this point to others not to gloss over it, but use His Word to show the certainty and seriousness and awfulness of this eternal consequence of being a sinner.

Which verse(s) would you use to explain this second point of the gospel? On the next page write out your plan for explaining this point.

For though I preach the gospel, I have nothing to glory of:
for necessity is laid upon me;
yea, woe is unto me, if I preach not the gospel!
1 Corinthians 9:16

May even the concept of
unreached peoples
be totally intolerable to us.

~ David Platt [7]

THE PUNISHMENT - DEATH

CHAPTER 12

THE CURE - CHRIST

Now comes the fun part of our message. The part filled with hope! This is also important not to rush through. The person must understand that Jesus is their ONLY hope!

This is how I explain this point.

For God so loved the world, that he gave his only begotten Son, that whosoever believeth in him should not perish, but have everlasting life. ~John 3:16

As I turn to John 3:16, I say, "By now, you may be wondering if there is any hope for you? Any hope for you to escape having to go to hell when you die? Well, let me tell you. God sent us here today to tell you that, 'Yes! There is hope!' His name is Jesus Christ.

So, Suzy, the third thing you must understand is that because God loved you so much, He sent His Son Jesus to take your punishment for you. (I then read the verse.)

God decided that He will accept Jesus' death as the sacrifice and payment for your sin, so that you don't have to perish in hell, separated from God forever! ...If you will believe that."

I then turn to 1 Corinthians 15:3-4 and say, "The Bible tells us in this verse..."

CHAPTER 12 - THE CURE

For I delivered unto you first of all that which I also received, how that Christ [Jesus] died for our sins according to the scriptures; And that he was buried, and that he rose again the third day according to the scriptures: ~1 Corinthians 15:3-4

"Jesus Christ is the Holy God who took on human flesh...so that He could die. He is God...in a man's body.

Since Jesus is God, He had no sin of his own to die for. Jesus Christ died for our sins. He died for your sins, Suzy. And not just some of them, but for ALL your sins—past, present, AND future. In fact, when Jesus died on the cross, ALL of your sins were future sins! Jesus died to pay for every sin you would ever commit.

Jesus was crucified on a cross and shed His blood to take your punishment for you.

So, Suzy, according to these verses, who did Christ die for?" She should respond..."He died for me." If she is still unsure, I'll show her again John 3:16. And tell her again, "Whosoever" includes anyone. Yes...even you, Suzy! No matter what you've done wrong in life. No matter who you are. Christ died for you!

Whisper that to your heart—'Christ died for me!' And believe it!" (I pause a minute for her to do that.)

"But notice that He didn't stay dead. He rose from the grave three days later, proving that God accepted His sacrifice as the payment for our sins, for your sins!

Now, Suzy, there are a couple more things to understand about Jesus—
First, Jesus says here..." (as you turn to John 14:6)

Jesus saith unto him, I am the way, the truth, and the life: no man cometh unto the Father, but by me. ~John 14:6

"Notice it says that Jesus is THE way...not A way. He is THE way...not one of many ways. In other words, Suzy, Jesus is the ONLY way to Heaven!

Second, you need to understand that **Jesus is THE way to Heaven...not *PART* of the way. It's not Jesus PLUS ... good works or church membership or baptism."**

For by grace are ye saved through faith; and that not of yourselves: it is the gift of God: Not of works, lest any man should boast.   ~Ephesians 2:8-9

"Remember, God requires death as the punishment for our sin. Right? Doing good works isn't the same as dying. Right? So, doing good works is not going to be acceptable to God as payment for our sins. Doing good works will never save us from our sin and the death in hell that we deserve."

I then ask this as a rhetorical question and immediately give the answer, pointing to the word "faith" in the verse—"So, what saves? Faith. Believing. Trusting Jesus and His death as your only hope of forgiveness and salvation from hell."

I then will explain faith here in this way—"Trusting God to save you from your sins and hell is kind of like when you go to sit on a chair. You don't try to sit on a chair that you don't have faith in to hold your weight. Right? So, if you trust that chair, you start to sit down. Until ALL your weight, your whole self, is resting in that chair. You are no longer making any effort to hold yourself up. The chair is doing ALL the work!

Trusting God for salvation involves placing ALL of yourself into God's hands (that chair) knowing He will keep you safe in His hands and take you into Heaven when you die. Because that is His promise in His Word. And God cannot lie!

You decide to stop thinking that you can hold yourself up and save yourself from hell (by your own good works or by belief in anything other than Jesus's death on the cross for you). And decide, rather, to completely rest in Jesus and His promise in His Word of forgiveness and eternal life."

WRAP-UP QUESTIONS -

"So, according to these verses, who is your only hope of salvation, the only One who can forgive you of your sins and save you from hell?"

(She should respond, "Jesus.")

"Again, what did Jesus do for you in order to save you? Is He still dead?"

(She should respond with something similar to—"He died on the cross to pay for my sins" and "No, He's alive." If she is unsure, then go back over these scriptures again. She must understand and believe these truths.)

"Is there anything you can do to save yourself from hell? Do your good works have anything to do with salvation?"

(She should respond with—"No" to both.)

If she answers with clear understanding, then I go on to tell her...
"That's right. So, Suzy, you now have a choice to make."

OTHER VERSES YOU MIGHT USE

To explain that Christ had no sin, but that He died for our sins, you might use Romans 5:8 and Matthew 28:6.

- **Romans 5:8 But God commendeth his love toward us, in that, while we were yet sinners, Christ died for us.**

Ask, "According to this verse, Suzy, who did Christ die for?" She should respond..."He died for me."

- **Matthew 28:6 He is not here: for he is risen, as he said. Come, see the place where the Lord lay.**

Be sure to explain that Jesus had no sin of His own to die for as I did above. And that He died for ALL of her sin. And that He did not stay dead.

Ask, "So, Suzy, according to these verses, who did Christ die for?" Then, "Is He still dead?"

Or, you could use Isaiah 53:5-6 and Matthew 28:6.

- ***Isaiah 53:5 But he was wounded for our transgressions, he was bruised for our iniquities: the chastisement of our peace was upon him; and with his stripes we are healed. All we like sheep have gone astray; we have turned every one to his own way; and the LORD hath laid on him the iniquity of us all.***

Explain that these verses refer to Jesus. That He died on the cross taking the punishment for our sins for us. That He had no sin of His own to die for. You might say, "Jesus died for my sins and for your sins, Suzy. He didn't die for some of your sins. He didn't just die for the sins you've done in the past, but for ALL of the sins you would ever commit in your life! *In fact, when Jesus died, ALL of your sins were future sins!* Also, notice here in Matthew 28:6 that He did not stay dead. Jesus rose from the dead and is now seated at the right hand of God the Father in Heaven." (Show her Matthew 28:6.)

To explain that it is Jesus and only Jesus, that we cannot earn our salvation, you could use Isaiah 64:6.

- ***Isaiah 64:6 But we are all as an unclean thing, and all our righteousnesses are as filthy rags; and we all do fade as a leaf; and our iniquities, like the wind, have taken us away.***

You might say something like, "Suzy, we needed Jesus to die for us, because we cannot be good enough to enter Heaven. Even the best good deeds we could think of to do would never measure up to God's perfect righteousness. In fact, our best good is as filthy rags compared to God and His perfect righteousness. And besides all that, doing good deeds was never the price God said would have to be paid for sin. Death has always been the penalty for sin. Either we must die for our sins ourselves, or else we can accept Jesus' death as the payment for our sins."

And ask the wrap-up questions—"So, according to these verses, Suzy, who is your only hope of salvation? What did Jesus do for you in order to save you? Is He still dead?"

OUTLINE FOR POINT #3
- There is hope in Jesus!
- God sent Jesus to die and take your punishment for you!
- Jesus is God and had no sin of His own. He died for our sins. ALL of them.
- Jesus did not stay dead. He is alive!
- Good works cannot save us. Only Jesus can.
- Explain how to be saved, what faith means.
- Ask the wrap-up questions.

PRAYER - Spend a few moments thanking God for teaching you how to share the gospel with those He has prepared to hear it. Ask Him to help you as you seek to learn all you can to be an effective messenger.

Decide which verses you would use to explain this point, and on the next page, write out what you would say for each one.

And let us not be weary in well doing:
for in due season we shall reap,
if we faint not.
~Galatians 6:9

THE CURE - CHRIST

CHAPTER 13

THE CHOICE - BELIEVE OR PERISH

Read Revelation 22:17. What invitation is repeated in this verse? Why do you think God repeats it?

This is where the wonder happens! Where a soul is born into the family and kingdom of God! This is where we issue the most incredible invitation God extends to us all...Come!

And saying, The time is fulfilled, and the kingdom of God is at hand: repent ye, and believe the gospel.
~Mark 1:15

This is where I say, "Suzy, you now have a choice to make. God says in Mark 1:15 that we must repent and believe the gospel. The gospel is all that I've just explained to you about Jesus and what He did for you by dying on the cross and rising from the dead."

WRAP-UP QUESTIONS -
"So, Suzy, will you repent of your sin? In other words, will you acknowledge to God that He is right and that you have been wrong; that you are sorry for your sin and want to live for Him; that you want and need Him and his forgiveness; ...and believe the gospel that Jesus died and rose again to pay for your sins for you?" She should respond, "Yes."

That if thou shalt confess with thy mouth the Lord Jesus, and shalt believe in thine heart that God hath raised him from the dead, thou shalt be saved. For with the heart man believeth unto righteousness; and with the mouth confession is made unto salvation.
~Romans 10:9-10

I then say, "You said you believed. Then according to these verses, what does God promise?" She should respond, "To save me." Then I ask, "Do you want Jesus to forgive you of your sins and save you from hell?" If she says, "Yes," I keep going.

For whosoever shall call upon the name of the Lord shall be saved.   ~Romans 10:13

"Calling on God means to pray. Praying is just talking to God like I'm talking to you right now. And telling Him what you want Him to do for you, like you just told me. In this verse right here, God promises that if you call upon Him, believing on Jesus, then He will save you. He will forgive you and save you from hell. You can take God at His Word. Because God cannot lie. Right? (Titus 1:2) So, believe His promise to save you, and just talk to Him.

I'll pray first. Then you pray in your own words...from your heart to Him. Tell Jesus you believe He died for you and ask Jesus to forgive you of your sins and save you from hell."

I then pray a very short prayer thanking God for Suzy and for her willingness to listen and believe what the Bible says about Jesus dying to pay for her sins for her. Then I pause with my head still bowed and eyes closed and wait for her to pray.

A Sinner's Prayer

Be really careful here. If you help someone pray, be sure to emphasize beforehand that it is NOT the words that save, but placing their faith solely in Jesus and the price He paid for them on the cross. You might also suggest that they think of God sitting on His throne in Heaven as they talk to Him. You do NOT want them solely focusing on repeating your words and not communicating with God!

I know, because that is exactly what I did. And left that "prayer" still unsaved. I knew nothing was different and sought out another person to ask about salvation. An hour later, alone in my bed, I prayed and talked to God from my heart and said, "Dear Jesus, please save me, and help me know I'm saved." And fell asleep before I could say, "Amen!" But that's all it took! Praise God! Just a simple heart-felt prayer.

Dear Jesus, please save me, and help me know I'm saved.

You could suggest the prayer I prayed, or you may want to lead them in a "sinner's prayer" such as this one -

Dear God, I know that I have sinned against You and deserve hell as my punishment. But I believe that Jesus your Son died and rose again to pay for my sins for me. Please forgive me and save my soul from hell. Thank You for Your wonderful gift of salvation and eternal life! Amen!

And wonder of wonders, another soul is born again! Oh, the wonder of it all! And the rejoicing in Heaven!

Read Luke 15:10. Who rejoices when each sinner comes to repentance?

If you want to have a part in rejoicing the heart of God, then let Him use you to bring souls to Himself. For the Father (and all Heaven) rejoices when a lost sinner is found!

What if the person says that they aren't ready to pray for salvation?

In that case, you might ask them, **"Is there something in particular keeping you from making that decision today?"** Maybe they feel that they have sinned too much for God to forgive them. Or, some other concern that you could help them put to rest. I've included a list of some common objections to the gospel in chapter 18 along with a verse that could help get them past that misunderstanding.

OUTLINE FOR POINT #4
- Explain that a choice must be made to change their destination from hell to heaven.
- Ask the wrap up questions, which also explain repentance.
- Recap God's promise to save. And that He cannot lie.
- Ask them if they want God to forgive and save them.
- Explain how to call on God for salvation.
- Pray a short prayer, then wait for them to pray.

PRAYER - Praise the Lord for saving souls every day. Ask Him to use you to bring joy to His heart.

Decide which verses you would use to explain this point, and on the next page, write out what you would say for each one.

*Likewise, I say unto you, there
is joy in the presence of the angels of
God over one sinner that repenteth.
~Luke 15:10*

THE CHOICE - BELIEVE OR PERISH

CHAPTER 14

THERE'S MORE!

Read Romans 8:38-39. What can separate believers from the love of God? List all the things that cannot separate believers from the love of God.

It is really important to explain a little further after someone prays for salvation, to help them have things settled in their mind.

ASSURANCE OF SALVATION

So, after a person prays for salvation, I ask them, while pointing to Romans 10:13, "Suzy, did you just call on the Lord?" She responds with, "Yes." And I then ask her, "Then according to this verse, what did Jesus just do for you?" She responds, "saved me."

And I tell her, "That's right. You did what God said you should. You believed on Jesus' death as the payment for your sins, and asked Jesus to save you. And since God cannot lie, He definitely did His part. Right? So, take God at His Word. And thank Him for saving you!"

ETERNAL SECURITY

It is also extremely important to cover this point, as well. This is where some come to fully realize that they are indeed saved.

To bring home the point of eternal security and help them see that they are completely and finally saved, I will ask, "Suzy, did you just get saved?" She responds, "Yes."

"So, let me ask you, if you sin next week, will you still be saved?" If you have adequately explained that Christ died and paid for ALL her sins in Point #3, then she should respond, "Yes."

If she is unsure, then I remind her that Jesus died for ALL of her sins, so He died for those she would commit next week, too. Then I ask, "So since Jesus died for ALL your sins, if you sin next week, will you still be saved?" She should then respond, "Yes."

It is wonderful to watch that understanding finally dawn on a person! I then ask, "What if you sin next year, will you still go to Heaven?" "Yes."

"What about 10 years from now? Will you still be saved and headed to Heaven, if you sin 10 years from now?" "Yes."

"That's right. Jesus paid for every one of your sins when He died on the cross. They are ALL taken care of. So, Suzy, if you died today, or 10 years from now, where would you go?" "Heaven."

And I give unto them eternal life; and they shall never perish, neither shall any man pluck them out of my hand. My Father, which gave them me, is greater than all; and no man is able to pluck them out of my Father's hand. I and my Father are one.
~John 10:28-30

Then I will add, "And you know what else, Suzy? The Bible says here in John 10:28 that when we get saved, we are in Jesus' hands, and nobody can take us out of His hands. Then it tells us that we are in the Father's hands, too, and nobody can take us out of His hands, either. Then the Bible tells us (in Ephesians 4:30) that we are sealed by the Holy Spirit.

So, it's like you're in Jesus' hand, inside the Father's hand, with the Holy Spirit wrapped all around!"

As I talk, I illustrate this point by placing one fist inside the other palm and say —"It's like if you wrapped my two hands all up tight with plastic wrap, only way better! God's hands and the Holy Spirit are way stronger than mine and this plastic wrap. So, do you think anything will be able to get you away from God, now that you belong to Him?"

OUTLINE FOR ASSURANCE AND SECURITY

- Assurance—
  - Review Romans 10:13.
- Eternal Security—
  - Ask whether they would still be saved if they sin in the future.
  - Tell them John 10:28 and illustrate how they are kept sealed in God's hands.

PRAYER - Aren't you so very thankful for the immutable truth of eternal security? So am I! Spend a few moments thanking God for this fact...that you will ALWAYS belong to Him! No. Matter. What.

On the next page write out how you would explain assurance and eternal security. Read it out loud several times.

For I am persuaded, that neither death, nor life,
nor angels, nor principalities, nor powers, nor
things present, nor things to come,
Nor height, nor depth, nor any other creature,
shall be able to separate us from the love of God,
which is in Christ Jesus our Lord.
~Romans 8:38-39

*To be a soul winner is the
happiest thing in this world.*

~ *Charles Spurgeon*[8]

ASSURANCE & SECURITY

CHAPTER 15

NOW WHAT?

Read again Matthew 28:19-20. What does verse 20 tell us we are to do once a person comes to faith in Christ?

The Great Commission tells us to not only make disciples by sharing the gospel message, but to also go on to disciple those who trust Christ as their Saviour. It is, therefore, our duty, once a disciple is made, to give them a little guidance on how to begin their new life in Christ. To answer for them the question, Now what?

My friend and late pastor's wife, April Decker, taught me this way to remember and explain the next steps of a new believer - G.R.O.W.

I begin this part of the conversation with something like -
"Congratulations, Suzy! I'm so happy to welcome you to the family of God! You are now my sister in Christ. And now that you belong to Jesus, He wants you to spend time getting to know Him and learning how to live in a way that pleases Him and brings joy to yourself. This is how we can remember what God wants us to do."

I hold up my hand and point to each of my four fingers as I say, "God wants us to grow in Him, to learn about Him and how to live for Him. G.R.O.W." Then I go on to explain each one.

G GO TO CHURCH
Pointing to my first finger, I say, "G stands for - Go to church."

"It is so important that we believers surround ourselves with others who know Jesus and can help us learn more about Him, too. Church gives us a place to do that."

"Church also gives us a place to worship God and to serve Him out of thankfulness for all He has done for us. Do you have a church you go to? If you don't, we would love for you to come to our church this Sunday." I will then tell them the service times and tell them about our bus ministry and/or offer to give them a ride myself."

R READ YOUR BIBLE
Pointing to my second finger, I go on to say, "R stands for - Read your Bible."

"It's very important that we spend some time alone with God every day to read His Word, the Bible, and to pray. Some people set aside time in the mornings, and others do it in the evening. My personal preference is the mornings before my day gets started. That way my heart and mind are strengthened by scripture before any of the day's problems and temptations have a chance to come at me. But either way, make it your new habit to get alone with God each day.

Start with prayer. Before you read your Bible, spend time talking to God about your life, your feelings, your concerns, your problems. Ask Him to guide you and give you wisdom. Tell Him about any needs you have and ask Him to provide. Tell Him how much you love Him and are thankful for all He does for you. And be sure to thank Him for hearing and answering your prayers. Finally, ask Him to open your heart and mind to understand what you are about to read in His Word that day.

Then open your Bible, and listen to God. The Bible contains all we need to know to live an abundant life, a successful Christian life. It is our instruction manual to show us how to live in a way that pleases and honors God and gives us peace and joy. (2 Timothy 3:16-17) I recommend that you start reading in the Book of John or in the Book of 1 John. Then go on to other books of the Bible."

I like to carry a Bible with me to give to each person who trusts Jesus as Saviour. I write the day's date in the Bible before I give it to them. The woman I talked to when I got saved did that for me, or I wouldn't know the date I got saved. And I'm glad I know that, not that knowing the date is all-important.

O OBEY GOD'S WORD
Pointing to my third finger, I say, "O stands for—Obey God's Word."

"The Bible tells us what pleases and displeases God. But there are many things you probably already know are right to do and wrong to do. So, whatever you know is right to do, do that. Whatever you know is wrong to do, ask God to help you stop doing.

That's another reason surrounding ourselves with other believers is helpful. They can help us by encouraging us and keeping us accountable in areas that are especially tempting for us. (1 Corinthians 15:33, Hebrews 3:13, Hebrews 10:24)

But your greatest help for living this life is God Himself. When you believed on Jesus, He sent His Spirit to live within your heart to guide you through this life. So, He is with you always to comfort, guide, and even convict you when you get off track and do something you shouldn't.

(NOTE—Be sure to include this part.) And when you fail. And you will. Remember that God is gracious and will forgive you. Just confess to Him and ask Him! (1 John 1:9) And keep on going, serving your Saviour, knowing that your sin cannot ever separate you from God's love! (Romans 8:38-39)

Just as you had to trust God to save your soul and give you eternal life, living your life here also requires you to trust God, to trust that He knows best. So, trust His commands to be for your good always, and then obey as best you can. Knowing that the Holy Spirit is with you to help you! God doesn't promise us an easy life, but He does promise to be with us and to help us through it, as we follow and obey Him."

W — WITNESS TO OTHERS
Pointing to my pinkie, I then say, "W stands for—Witness to others."

"Now that you know the way to Heaven, God wants you to tell others so that they can know, too! The easiest way to get started is to go tell someone who already knows Jesus. Do you know someone you could tell? Maybe your mom or a brother or sister or a friend?" I pause for their answer, then I say, "Ok, good. Then as soon as I leave, you go tell them what happened to you today! They will be so excited for you!

The next easiest way to witness to others about the way to Heaven is to obey Jesus' command to be baptized. To do that, you would need to talk with your pastor about your decision today to trust Jesus as your Saviour and tell him that you want to be baptized.

Remember, baptism doesn't have anything to do with your salvation. It is simply an act of obedience and a witness to others that you now belong to God."

"Baptism is a picture of what Jesus did for us when He died on the cross. When you stand with your pastor in the water, that pictures Jesus hanging on the cross dying for you. (I hold up my arm with my elbow bent and my hand pointing upward.) When you go under the water, that pictures Jesus' burial. (I rotate my arm backwards to illustrate the person lying back in the water.) When you are raised up out of the water, that pictures Jesus' resurrection from the dead and His victory over death and hell for you! (I rotate my arm back upright.) Symbolically, you are raised to walk in Jesus' victory in newness of life. (Romans 6:3-4)

As you grow in your knowledge of the Bible, you will learn what Bible verses are helpful in explaining to someone else how to be saved. But until then, you can always witness to others by simply telling them how you came to understand that you needed forgiveness and salvation. Tell them about Jesus and what He did for you by dying on the cross, and how you believed on His death and resurrection as your only hope of salvation from hell. Then tell them that they can, too! God will be honored. And so pleased."

PLAN TO FOLLOW-UP

Finally, I plan a follow-up visit for the next week. I tell her that I want to bring her a booklet for new Christians that she could read and work through. When I deliver the booklet, I offer to help her with it to see if she'd like me to visit with her again.

Sometimes I have chosen to give the person my email address so that they can email me any questions they might have about our visit that day or about the Bible as they read. I also point out our church information on the tract I gave.

Next Thursday 6:30 p.m. !!

OUTLINE FOR 'NOW WHAT?'

- G—Go to church.
- R—Read your Bible, praying first.
- O—Obey, doing what you already know is right.
- W—Witness.
  - Tell another believer today.
  - Tell their pastor and be baptized.
  - Explain baptism.
  - Tell others about what Jesus did for them.
- Plan a follow-up visit.

PRAYER - Spend a few moments thanking God for as many people as you can remember who have played a part in helping you grow as a believer over the years. Ask God to use you as that person in someone else's life, helping them along in their journey of faith.

Think about how you would help a brand-new believer know what she/he should do next as they begin their new life in Christ. On the next page write out how you would explain the believer's first steps.

We should be holy people eager
to greet our Lord when He returns,
ready at any moment for the trumpet's call,
people of optimism, busy in evangelism,
hands to the plow, eyes on the prize.

~ *David Jeremiah* [9]

G.R.O.W.

CHAPTER 16

ALL TOGETHER NOW!

When we talk to someone to share the gospel we don't want to come across as reciting a sermon we've memorized. I've given you my plan, and that's what it is...a plan. Instead of memorizing my plan word for word, I memorized the verses I'd use and the points I'd want to cover for each one. But being familiar with a full conversation helps me kind of know what to say when I'm going through the plan with someone.

My plan may seem pretty long to you right now. But as you get comfortable with what to say for each point, you will find that it doesn't take as long to talk through it with someone as you might think.

One of the things I've found helpful is to put the outline of my plan on my phone in my OneNote app. Just knowing it's there helps. I always review it and talk through it just before I head out to go soul winning. And sometimes I've glanced at it as we've walked from house to house.

I've included my outline on the next page for you to use as a reference in making your own. **Or, you may photo copy it, or type it into your Note app, and use it for your own personal soul-winning efforts. In fact, please do!**

PRAYER - Thank the Lord for giving you the time, and helping you, to write out a plan to share the gospel with others. Ask Him to help you review and practice your plan regularly so that you are ready for those open doors He has for you.

Use the page provided to make an outline, or some kind of abbreviated list, of your notes. Or, use mine. And read/talk through it a couple of times.

The Gospel Message

- **The Problem—Sin**
  Rom 5:12—where sin came from; what sin is; all have sinned; Stolen? Unkind? Lied? **Then according to this verse and your own admission, what are you?**
- **The Punishment—Death**
  Rom 5:12—result of sin; all die physically; there is a 2nd death, a spiritual death
  Rev 21:8—2nd death in hell in lake of fire; soul separated from God and light and goodness and love—**You've admitted you've lied and sinned. Then according to this verse, where are you headed?**
  Matt 25:46—everlasting punishment, no escape, no hope
- **The Cure—Christ**
  Is there any hope? Yes!
  Jn 3:16—Because God loved you so much He sent His Son Jesus to take your punishment for you. God decided that He will accept Jesus' death as the sacrifice and payment for your sin, so you don't have to perish in hell forever! ...If you will believe that.
  1 Cor 15:3-4—Christ had no sin of his own; God in a man's body; Christ died for our sins; ALL your sins—past, present, & future; crucified on a cross and shed His blood; took your punishment for you—**According to this verse, who did Christ die for?** Get them to say "He died for me." Notice Jesus didn't stay dead. He is alive today!
  Jesus, and only Jesus—Jesus plus nothing
  - Jn 14:6—Jesus is the way to heaven. Jesus is THE way, not A way. THE way, not one of many ways.
  - Eph 2:8-9—Jesus is THE way, not PART of the way. Not Jesus PLUS ... good works or church membership or baptism. What saves? faith, believing, trusting Jesus and His death as your only hope of salvation from hell.
  According to these verses, who is your only hope of salvation, the only One who can forgive you of your sins and save you from hell? Again, what did Jesus do for you in order to save you? Is He still dead?
- **The Choice—Repent and believe...or Perish**
  You now have a choice to make.
  Mk 1:15b—**Will you repent of your sin? Will you acknowledge to God that He is right and that you have been wrong; that you are sorry for your sin and want to live for Him; that you want and need Him and his forgiveness; ...and believe that Jesus died to pay for your sins for you?**
  YES—Rom 10:9-10 You said you believed. Then according to these verses, what does God promise?
  Rom 10:13—I'll pray first, then you pray in your own words telling Jesus you believe He died for you and asking Jesus to forgive your sin and save your soul from hell.
- **Assurance**—Did you just call on the Lord? **Then according to this verse, what did Jesus do for you?** Take God at His Word.
- **Eternal security**—cannot lose salvation—Eph 2:8-9, Jn 10:28-29
  GROW—Public profession/baptism—Acts 2:41, Matt 28:19-20, Rom 10:11, Acts 8:38 (illustrate immersion)

The Gospel Message

CHAPTER 17

OPEN DOORS

I used to feel rushed when seeking to share the gospel with someone. As if I had to get it all out before the person lost interest and ended the conversation. But not anymore.

It was around 10:15 on a Saturday morning when Janet and I met Shondra. She opened the door with the cutest little 7-month-old baby girl on her hip. God further opened the door for me to go inside with Shondra and help her understand about how she, too, could be 100% sure she would go to Heaven. Janet waited outside so that our group would know where I was.

Shondra and I talked for at least 25 minutes seated in her den. The whole time I talked and showed her the scriptures, Shondra held the baby. Her husband was in their kitchen that was open to the den, eating cereal and watching the TV that was playing in the den...again, where we sat talking.

But Shondra stayed glued to what I was saying. And the baby stayed as happy as could be.

To the Lord's glory, Shondra wanted to pray and receive Jesus as her Saviour! So, I held the baby while she prayed.

As I was leaving, at around 11:00 a.m., Shondra mentioned that she was about to go feed her baby breakfast! I couldn't believe it! With all the distractions, God kept the door open for Shondra to become His child! Then when I realized that the baby had not even eaten yet and was still so happy, I knew God had just taught me another truly freeing soul-winning lesson.

When God opens a door, *nothing* can shut it!

So, I need not feel rushed. I can calmly explain each point, because if God's Spirit has opened the door, it will stay open. And I need not be worrying about the time, or anything else, but rather making sure I explain each point clearly and thoroughly enough that the person understands the basis for their faith in Jesus!

PRAYER - Thank the Lord for giving you His Spirit to help and guide you in seeking the lost for Christ. Ask Him to help you to simply seek open doors, and once you find one, to calmly and slowly and clearly present the gospel to that soul.

PREPARE YOUR BIBLE - Another help I use besides my OneNote app (mentioned in chapter 16) is having tabs on my soul winner's Bible that I use. You might want to take time today and mark your Bible either with tabs or by making a reference chain to help you know what verse to go to next. Start at the first verse in your plan and in the margin beside that verse, write the reference to the next verse in your plan until you get to the last verse.

Go back and practice following your chain all the way through your gospel plan. It's important to practice using your Bible to go through the plan. If you've made any mistake in your labeling, it's best to discover it now!

> *I know thy works: behold,*
> *I have set before thee an open door,*
> *and no man can shut it: for thou hast a*
> *little strength, and hast kept my word,*
> *and hast not denied my name.*
> *~Revelation 3:8*

We have all eternity to celebrate the victories but only a few hours before sunset to win them.

~ Amy Carmichael[10]

CHAPTER 18

COMMON OBJECTIONS

Remember, in chapter 7 we talked about how it's God's job to open doors. Our job is simply to look for the open doors. If at any time in my conversation with Shondra she had become disinterested or had begun to ask off-topic questions, then I would have realized that she was not the open door I was looking for that day. In that case, what I would need to do is maybe answer, as best I could, a couple of her questions, and then make my exit.

To go and keep looking for the doors God had opened and made ready to hear.

Sometimes people do ask some really crazy questions or mention some objection they have to God, religion, or the Bible, so it's good to continue learning how we can answer some of those concerns. Maybe that is the one obstacle that is standing in the way of their belief. If you can answer it, do so, and try to get the conversation back on track with your gospel plan. But don't try to force the conversation, because it is God's work to make them ready to hear.

I've included in this chapter a list of possible objections people may express and a scripture reference that you could share to help them. But don't worry about learning them right away. Because our ultimate goal when out soul winning is to look for the open doors. Right now just concentrate on learning and sharing your soul-winning plan.

I've learned how to respond to some of these objections in my list as I've been out soul winning and come across people who clearly were not ready to listen to the gospel. For example, one day another friend and I and my girls were out soul winning and met a middle-aged man wearing all-leather biker gear. He was a tall man and pretty intimidating looking. When I gave him a tract and asked him "the question," he responded, "I don't believe in religion. In this country we have freedom to choose." And ranted on some more. So, we "Uh huh'd" a few times and quickly left.

I was stumped. What could I have said to him?

Well, later that day, the Holy Spirit brought John 3:36 to mind. The Lord showed me that I could have cued on his use of the word "choice" and used this verse to tell him—"You are so right, Sir. We do have a choice about where we go when we die. John 3:36 says... God has given us the choice to believe on His Son's death for us for the payment of our sins, or to not believe. We can choose to have everlasting life, or we can choose to continue living under the wrath of God and die and spend eternity in hell. It is our choice. God won't force His gift of salvation from hell on anyone."

Another time, I met a man who said "There's all kinds of religions out there. How do you know yours is right?" Again, I was stumped. And again, as I thought and prayed about what I could have said, the Spirit later brought to mind Acts 4:12. I could have quoted this verse to him and told him that the Bible says that salvation from hell comes only through Jesus, the Son of God.

I could also quote John 14:6 and tell him briefly that Jesus died to pay for his sins for him and ask him to read the tract I had given him.

I could also have quoted John 7:17. I could have then told him that God wants him to know the truth, whether what I'm telling him is from God or just something I've made up. And that if he seriously wants to know the truth, then God will show him. All he has to do is be willing to act on that truth when God shows him. Because if he's not going to do what God shows him *is* the truth, then why should God show him?

I learned through this trial-and-error method for several years until I finally thought, "Man, I wish I could hear the Spirit tell me what to say while I'm still *with* the person!"

So, I prayed for that. And the Lord has been helping me more to hear Him in the moment, now that I'm also not worried about being rushed when presenting the gospel.

He that believeth on the Son hath everlasting life: and he that believeth not the Son shall not see life; but the wrath of God abideth on him.
~John 3:36

Neither is there salvation in any other: for there is none other name under heaven given among men, whereby we must be saved.
~Acts 4:12

If any man will do his will, he shall know of the doctrine, whether it be of God, or whether I speak of myself.
~John 7:17

CHAPTER 18 - COMMON OBJECTIONS

Having a plan and learning that I don't have to rush the presentation has helped me to relax and be able to hear God as I share the gospel message. My time with Jack that I shared about in chapter 10 is an example of one such time.

So, in conclusion, it does get easier the more you keep going, keep talking with people, and keep trying...and keep listening for what God will teach you!

PRAYER - Thank the Lord that His Word has the answer to any objection man can come up with concerning faith in Jesus. Ask the Lord to help you keep learning and growing as a witness for Him. Thank Him again for His willingness to teach you and to use you in His work of saving souls from hell.

Read through your plan again out loud a couple of times. You will need to do this each day until you get really comfortable with your plan. Then try it out on a family member or friend.

You might also check out the list of common objections to the gospel on the next page.

CHAPTER 18 - COMMON OBJECTIONS

LIST OF COMMON OBJECTIONS TO THE GOSPEL

- There are too many hypocrites in the church.
    Jeremiah 2:5, Romans 5:8
- There are many religions.
    Acts 4:12, John 14:6
- God is too good to send people to hell.
    Romans 2:4-5
- If God is good, then why do bad things happen to good people?
    Isaiah 55:8-9, Romans 9:20
- The Christian life is too hard.
    Matthew 11:30, Psalms 16:11, Proverbs 13:15
- I cannot give up my bad habits or evil ways.
    Galatians 6:7-8, Philippians 4:13, Luke 13:3
- I am afraid I can't live the Christian life (too weak).
    1 Corinthians 10:13, Philippians 4:13
- I am seeking Christ but cannot find Him.
    Jeremiah 29:13, Luke 19:10, John 7:17
- I am too great a sinner.
    1 Timothy 1:15, Romans 5:6-8, emphasize "whosoever" in John 3:16 &
    John 6:37 (Yes, your sins are great, but they have all been settled.)

John 3:36 (It's not trying, feelings, or works, but **believing** that saves.)
- I'm a good person.
- I'm trying to be good. I do good things.
- I don't feel like I'm lost. I feel like I'm going to heaven.
- I belong to fill-in-the-blank church, so I'm good.

Mark 8:36, Matthew 6:32-33 (objections related to loss)
- I will be persecuted.
- My business will suffer.
- I will lose my friends.
- I will have to give up too much.
- I love the world too much.

2 Corinthians 6:2 (objections related to time)
- It's too late for me.
- Not now. I'll get saved later.
- I'm too young/old.
- I'm waiting for God's time.

We do not fail in our evangelism if we faithfully tell the gospel to someone who is not subsequently converted; we fail only if we do not faithfully tell the gospel at all.

~ Mark Dever[11]

CHAPTER 19

A TURTLE, A TICKET, AND TEENAGERS

It was a Monday evening around dusk on a winding deserted country road when suddenly I saw a turtle in the middle of my lane! I swerved to miss it. And you guessed it. I ran right over it! I couldn't look back; I was so upset. Poor little (rather large, really) guy.

But I pressed on, because you see, there were a lot of teenaged boys, along with my church group, counting on me being at the services that night at the Juvenile Facility. I'd made a commitment and needed to keep it.

As I drove into the parking lot, however, I noticed that things didn't look right. I couldn't locate any vehicles I recognized. Then it dawned on me after a few minutes...I must have missed a very important memo. The facility, I learned later, had canceled church services due to it being the 4th of July!

So, I made my way out of the parking lot and headed home, only to be stopped by a policeman as I was entering the city limit! You'd have to know this road to understand what happened. And yep, he gave me a ticket! My first ever! And my only, ever! But I was speeding, and so had broken the law and deserved a ticket. So, it's all good, and lesson learned.

But at the time, even knowing I deserved it, I was so upset with myself. I cried all the way home. Here I was trying to serve the Lord, and I run over and kill an innocent turtle and get a speeding ticket. And for what? So, that I could go to a canceled service!

My point? Serving the Lord in any capacity doesn't always go as planned or run smoothly.

Oh, the stories I could tell. For instance, ...

One Monday night at the Juvenile Facility we had just started the service when I suddenly found myself being practically lifted by the missionary who led our group and pushed to the back of the room where he blocked me from sight. It all happened so fast that I was just a little confused instead of being scared out of my mind, thankfully. A nasty fight had suddenly erupted between two of the boys. The guards were fast enough that the situation was diffused, and the boys taken away, rather quickly.

Who says it's boring to serve the Lord?!

I witnessed a milder bit of violence on another occasion. Sadly, the gospel has that effect on some folks.

One morning after dropping Taylor, my oldest daughter, off at school, my four-year-old daughter and I went by the grocery store to get a few things. While there, I started giving a tract to those I passed in the aisles. Well, Mallory asked if she could have some to give, too. So, I gave her 3 at a time. We rounded the end of one aisle and started down the next when I spotted her next target. A man wearing an outfit that was all black with a bit of white showing on the front of his collar.

Immediately I thought, "Oh, boy, she's gonna want to give him one, and I'm not sure if he'll be OK with it." Sure enough, "Mama, I want to give him one." "Ok, sweetheart." I mean, this was a teaching moment. I couldn't tell her, "No, we can only give tracts to certain people."

So, she walked up to him and looking way up at him, handed him the tract and told him in her small little girl voice that she wanted to give it to him to read today. Well, you'd think she'd handed him a snake as fast as he ripped the tract in half and threw it in my buggy! Then getting in my personal space, he began to rant and curse. Yes, curse. I kid you not.

In that moment, the Holy Spirit gave me what to say. Normally, I might would have tried to address some of the things he said, but the Spirit led me to simply ask, "Sir, are you cursing?" That stopped him for a split second as he considered what I'd just said. But then he just blustered on until he left soon after.

Thankfully, there was a lady waiting at the end of the aisle who witnessed the whole thing and helped me to feel safe. I gave her a tract and said, "You know if someone didn't agree with my opinion, I certainly don't think cursing at them would help them see my point of view." She agreed. And I believe she probably read that tract that day. I can't help but believe God was all in that encounter working His purposes.

Soul winning won't always be easy or rewarded in the ways we might think. But it is always worth it! And will be rewarded in the life to come...and for all eternity!

You may not see loads of numbers of people accept Christ as Saviour due to your efforts to share the gospel. I haven't. But I have seen some. And so, will you. And who knows, maybe there will be more souls in Heaven because of our efforts than we will ever know about until we get there. I'm hoping and praying that there will be many surprises for me in Heaven, people who got saved that I didn't know about here in this life. Wouldn't that be such a wonderful surprise?!

PRAYER - Spend a few moments reading and praying through the Soul-Winning Promises in Chapter 5. Let God's words fill your soul with overflowing joy and thankfulness. Ask the Lord to give you souls for the Saviour now, as well as, many surprises in Heaven one day.

> *There have been times of late*
> *when I have had to hold on to*
> *one text with all my might:*
> *"It is required in stewards that*
> *a man be found faithful."*
> *Praise God, it does*
> *not say "sucessful."*
>
> *~ Amy Carmichael[12]*

CHAPTER 20

THIS MAKES THE DIFFERENCE!

Read Acts 16:27-31. When the jailer discovers that the prisoners have not escaped, what does he do?

Of all the people the Lord has used me to lead to Him, only two of those approached me.

The first was many years ago. While out running errands, I got a phone call about a seven-year-old little boy, Joey, who had told his guardian that he wanted to be saved. His guardian wanted someone who'd worked with children to help Joey. So, he contacted the lady who called me, asking if I would talk to Joey. I still remember talking with Joey and showing him the scriptures and watching him pray for Jesus to save him. Such a sweet memory!

The second was my youngest daughter. When she was eight years old, she came to my room one night wanting to talk to me about her salvation. She meant business with God that night. I praise the Lord for allowing me to be there to share the gospel with my sweet little girl and hear her pray for Jesus to save her! What a most precious memory!

Read Acts 8:29-31. How is it that the eunuch came to meet Phillip that day?

If you're like me, you'd rather wait and let those who want to hear the gospel come to you. However, very rarely will anyone approach you and ask you how to be saved.

We must find them. We must, like Philip, be prepared to heed the Spirit's promptings and GO. We must be Christ-like, and like Christ, "be about my[our] Father's business"—the business of seeking the lost. (Luke 2:49, 19:10)

My point?

Doors don't move. We must. We have to approach the door. And knock. And be ready to walk through the open doors with confident faith in our God who is still not willing that any should perish. (2 Peter 3:9)

Learning to witness takes want to, conviction of hell, faith in our saving God, prayer, and lots of practice! But is so worth all the effort, for the harvest is plenteous. So many need to hear.

Then saith he unto his disciples,
The harvest truly is plenteous,
but the labourers are few;
Pray ye therefore the Lord of the
harvest, that he will send forth
labourers into his harvest.

~Matthew 9:37-38

Learning to be an effective witness for the Saviour also takes faithfulness. It takes a committed faithfulness to our Saviour to keep praying, preparing, and presenting the gospel message day after day, even when we don't get to see the results of our labour.

But remember, all God asks, or rather, requires, of us is to be faithful stewards. To faithfully share the gospel message. (1 Corinthians 4:2) If you do that, then you ARE an effective witness of the Lord Jesus Christ!

Read Romans 10:14. How does a person get to the place of being able to call on the Lord for salvation?

CHAPTER 20 - THIS MAKES THE DIFFERENCE!

God has chosen us His people through which to share the gospel message in order to save souls. There is a progression. Someone tells. The person hears. And then believes and is saved.

So, dear reader, what makes the difference between Heaven and Hell for the souls God means to use you to reach with the gospel message?

You do! YOU make the difference!

You being about your Father's business.

Will you be that faithful, faith-filled vessel God can use? Will you go? Will you look for the open doors waiting just for you?

O.K. now, let's make it real. Fill in your answers as your commitment.

There are many places that we can go to look for open doors. We can give a gospel tract and ask our open-door question anywhere there are people! But here are a few suggestions—the grocery store, the shopping mall, the doctor's office waiting room, restaurants, your neighborhood, your church visitation/soul-winning ministry, other church ministries, the county fair, the state fair, the park.

Where will you look this week?

How many tracts will you commit to giving this week?
(Remember, it's O.K. to start small. Look back at Chapter 2 again for some suggestions on how to get started giving tracts.)

How many times will you commit to asking the open-door question this week?

PRAYER - Tell the Lord about your commitment to give the gospel this week. Thank Him for His goodness and mercy on your soul. And ask Him to give you *a confident, courageous faith* to keep your commitment to Him to *share His gospel message this week...and for the rest of your life!*

Life is short. Let's make it count!

Also I heard the voice of the Lord, saying,
Whom shall I send, and who will go for us?
Then said I,

Here am I; send me.

~ Isaiah 6:8

REFERENCES

1) Frank Jenner. (2020). Retrieved November 7, 2020, from
https://en.wikipedia.org/wiki/Frank_Jenner
2) Smethurst, D. (March, 2004). That white-haired man on George Street. *Grace and Truth Magazine.*
https://www.gtpress.org/gtweb/gtmag/mag04/mar04/serving.html
3) Halverson, R. (n.d.). *Richard Halverson quotes and sayings – page 1.*
https://www.inspiringquotes.us/author/5825-richard-halverson
4) Strobel, L. (n.d.). *Lee Strobel quotes and sayings – page 1.*
https://www.inspiringquotes.us/author/5698-lee-strobel
5) Pippert, R. (n.d.). *Rebecca Pippert quotes.*
https://libquotes.com/rebecca-pippert
6) Nimeskern, J. (n.d.). *Hell's first moment...throughout eternity.*
http://www.biblebelievers.com/Nimeskern1.html
7) Platt, D. (n.d.). *David Platt quotes and sayings – page 1.*
https://www.inspiringquotes.us/author/5358-david-platt
8) Spurgeon, C. (n.d.). *Charles Spurgeon quote.*
https://libquotes.com/charles-spurgeon/quote/lbt6r4h
9) Jeremiah, D. (n.d.). *David Jeremiah quotes.*
https://loveexpands.com/quotes/david-jeremiah-1093343/
10) Carmichael, A. (n.d.). *Amy Carmichael quotes and sayings – page 1.*
https://www.inspiringquotes.us/author/5477-amy-carmichael
11) Dever, M. (n.d.) *Mark Dever quotes and sayings – page 1.*
https://www.inspiringquotes.us/author/8359-mark-dever
12) Carmichael, A. (n.d.). *Amy Carmichael quotes and sayings – page 2.*
https://www.inspiringquotes.us/author/5477-amy-carmichael/page:2

AUTHOR'S NOTE

A Special Thank You! & Request

What did you think? But first,

THANK YOU!

Thank you so much for purchasing this book, *Through Open Doors: Unlocking the Mystery of Soul Winning*! I pray that the Lord has used it in a very real way in your growth as His disciple.

If you enjoyed reading this book and found it helpful, I hope that you might take a few moments to post a review on Amazon. I do read every review, and they help me in many ways. But more importantly, your review could be used to encourage others to also purchase and begin their journey toward becoming the soul winner God wants them to be!

For convenience, here is the direct link to the Amazon review page for *Through Open Doors: Unlocking the Mystery of Soul Winning >>*

http://www.amazon.com/review/create-review?&asin=1647752701

And if you have already left a review...Thank You!! You are awesome!

Many Blessings!

Teresa

For more information and to purchase the paperback or a pdf file >>
https://www.ladiesdrawingnigh.org/through-open-doors-soul-winning/

www.ingramcontent.com/pod-product-compliance
Lightning Source LLC
Chambersburg PA
CBHW081513040426
42447CB00013B/3216